Housing in Suburban Employment Centers

Development Opportunities and Constraints

Nina J. Gruen
Gruen Gruen + Associates

Richard C. Ward and Barry Hogue
Development Strategies, Inc.

G. Ronald Witten
M/PF Research, Inc.

Richard B. Peiser, Kenneth Beck, Glenn Hickman, and Timothy Siegel
The Lusk Center for Real Estate Development, University of Southern California

Beth E. Williams
Research, Education, and Publications, ULI–the Urban Land Institute

Urban Land Institute

About ULI–the Urban Land Institute

ULI–the Urban Land Institute is a nonprofit education and research institute that is supported and directed by its members. Its mission is to provide responsible leadership in the use of land to enhance the total environment.

ULI sponsors educational programs and forums to encourage an open international exchange of ideas and sharing of experience; initiates research that anticipates emerging land use trends and issues and proposes creative solutions based on that research; provides advisory services; and publishes a wide variety of materials to disseminate information on land use and development.

Established in 1936, the Institute today has some 13,000 members and associates from more than 40 countries representing the entire spectrum of the land use and development disciplines. They include developers, builders, property owners, investors, architects, public officials, planners, real estate brokers, appraisers, attorneys, engineers, financiers, academics, students, and librarians. ULI members contribute to higher standards of land use by sharing their knowledge and experience. The Institute has long been recognized as one of the country's most respected and widely quoted sources of objective information on urban planning, growth, and development.

Richard M. Rosan
Executive Vice President

Project Staff

Senior Vice President,
Research, Education, and Publications
Rachelle L. Levitt

Vice President/Publisher
Frank H. Spink, Jr.

Project Director
Lloyd W. Bookout

Senior Fellow
J. Thomas Black

Managing Editor
Nancy H. Stewart

Manuscript Editor
Barbara M. Fishel/Editech

Book Design/Layout
Helene Y. Redmond
HYR Graphics

Production Manager
Diann Stanley-Austin

Recommended bibliographic listing:
Nina J. Gruen et al. *Housing in Suburban Employment Centers: Development Opportunities and Constraints.* Washington, D.C.: ULI–the Urban Land Institute, 1995.

ULI Catalog Number: H03
International Standard Book Number: 0-87420-765-7
Library of Congress Catalog Card Number: 95-60827

Contents

Introduction 1

Chapter 1. The Case for Housing in Suburban Employment Centers 2
Beth E. Williams, ULI–the Urban Land Institute
Characteristics of the Suburban Employment Center 3
The Evolution of the Suburban Employment Center 4
Housing Supply and Demand in SECs 4
The Case for Housing 7
Conclusion 9

Chapter 2. Case Study: Walnut Creek, California 12
Nina J. Gruen, Gruen Gruen + Associates, San Francisco, California
Organization of the Case Study 12
The Metamorphosis of an Edge City 13
Restraints on Housing Development 18
The Effect of the Mismatch between Commercial and Residential Development 23
Lost and Remaining Opportunities 28

Chapter 3. Case Study: City Centre, Southfield, Michigan 32
Richard C. Ward and Barry Hogue, Development Strategies, Inc., St. Louis, Missouri
Introduction 32
Southfield's Evolution 34
Current and Projected Demand for Higher-Density Housing 38
Supply of Higher-Density Housing 42
Development Potential and Implementation Strategies 43

Chapter 4. Case Study: Galleria Area, Dallas, Texas 46
G. Ronald Witten, M/PF Research, Inc., Dallas, Texas
Introduction 46
The Galleria Area: Current Status and Critical Trends 47
The Housing Market in the Galleria Area 53
Forecast of Housing Demand in the Galleria Area 55
Identification of the Development Site 57
Constraints on the Development Site 57
Summary 59

Chapter 5. Case Study: South Coast Town Center, Orange County, California 62
*Richard B. Peiser, Kenneth Beck, Glenn Hickman, and Timothy Siegel, The Lusk Center for
Real Estate Development, University of Southern California, Los Angeles, California*
Executive Summary 62
Introduction 64
Metropolitan and Historical Context 65
The Potential Demand for Housing in the Selected Area 75
The Supply Side: Past Experience and Projected Capacity 84
Alternative Strategies for Increasing Housing in and around South Coast Town Center 93
General Conclusions 97

Chapter 6. Conclusion 100

ULI Review Committee

About the Contributors

Nina J. Gruen is executive vice president/principal sociologist at San Francisco–based **Gruen Gruen + Associates** (GG + A), a firm of economists and market analysts providing research and consulting in land use policy. Since its founding in 1970, GG + A has pioneered the use of economic, social, and fiscal impact analysis. GG + A impact studies have accurately and comprehensively portrayed the effects of public and private real estate developments, land use plans, regulations, annexations, and assessments on treasuries, taxpayers, consumers, other residents, and property owners.

Richard C. Ward is president and **Barry Hogue** is principal of **Development Strategies, Inc.**, a St. Louis–based consulting firm providing research, planning, and counseling in real estate and community and economic development. The firm's consulting services include economic, market, and attitudinal research, land use and facilities planning, and real estate counseling and appraisal.

G. Ronald Witten is president of **M/PF Research, Inc.**, a market research consulting firm specializing in analysis of real estate markets nationwide. Based in Dallas, M/PF works for builders, developers, lenders, and investors in evaluating market opportunities for acquisition and development of housing and commercial and mixed-use properties.

Richard B. Peiser is director of **The Lusk Center for Real Estate Development** at the University of Southern California (USC), **Kenneth Beck** is an instructor at USC and owner of the Kenneth Beck Company, and **Glenn Hickman** and **Timothy Siegel** are students in the Master of Real Estate Development program at USC. As the outreach arm of USC's Master of Real Estate Development program, the Center is devoted to research and the ongoing study of real estate development through a variety of programs, seminars, and workshops, and serves as a liaison between the academic program and the real estate development industry. Using both the university's educational resources and the talents of industry leaders, the Center is able to offer public programs addressing the interests of practitioners and students and to foster excellence in the field of real estate development.

Beth E. Williams is an associate in the research, education, and publications department at **ULI–the Urban Land Institute**, where she conducts research on a variety of land use and development issues. She served as project associate for the 1995 edition of *ULI Market Profiles* and is responsible for ULI's MetroPackets series.

Introduction

It is commonly believed that most future commercial and retail development will take place in developing suburban employment centers outside central cities. But already many of these suburban centers are being choked by highway systems that cannot support the increased traffic. In response to concerns about traffic and other development-related impacts, some local jurisdictions have begun to limit new development in and around large employment centers, tending to focus such efforts on housing because of the favorable tax advantages associated with retail and commercial uses.

Ironically, limiting the development of housing within commercial and employment centers has been shown over the past decade to worsen traffic conditions by forcing employees to commute longer distances to and from work. Some government jurisdictions—particularly regional planning agencies—are now arguing that housing in job-rich areas should be encouraged as part of larger traffic plans to improve the physical relationship between jobs and housing. Providing high-density residential units within the mix of housing can also encourage the local supply of labor by offering the full range of wages and skills required by the activity center's growing economy.

The purpose of the case studies in this volume is to establish whether specific local conditions influence the opportunities and constraints for higher-density housing. Four activity centers across the United States were selected on the basis of their differing geography, access by public transit and automobile, entitlement environments, amount of built versus unbuilt space, and housing and employment demands. Specifically, each case study was to identify the housing demand that could be produced within the local housing market, assess the degree to which this potential demand is being met in the immediate area serving the suburban employment center, identify obstacles or incentives to the supply of higher-density housing near these employment centers, and specify the local policy issues that have supported these obstacles or incentives. In each case study, the consultant evaluated the degree to which developers and communities have been successful in capitalizing on the potential demand for higher-density housing resulting from the employment center's concentration of workers.

Underlying all of the case studies is the premise that compelling reasons exist for encouraging higher-density housing in and around suburban employment centers:
▼ Reduced commuting times;
▼ Reduced auto emissions;
▼ More efficient use of land;
▼ Increased housing choices;
▼ Increased affordable housing;
▼ Expanded development opportunities;
▼ Increased residential density to support downtown retailing and services; and
▼ The potential for adding vitality and activity to suburban employment centers that are too often deserted after working hours.

This research effort was launched under the direction of J. Thomas Black, ULI senior fellow. ULI appreciates his efforts in defining and initiating the research as well as those of the authors who wrote the four case studies.

Chapter 1

▲ ▲ ▲ ▲ ▲ ▲ ▲ ▲ ▲ ▲

The Case For Housing In Suburban Employment Centers

by
Beth E. Williams

ULI–the Urban Land Institute

The nature of the metropolitan landscape in the United States has changed radically over the last five decades. The notion that a central city core would forever serve as a primary place of industry, employment, residential life, and leisure activity has become outdated. The boundaries of our traditional city centers have expanded into areas once known only as suburban bedroom communities, and recent trends in economic activity, fueled by vastly improved transportation and communications technology, have served as the driving forces behind the emergence of a relatively new phenomenon—*the suburban employment center.*

The suburban employment center (SEC) is generally characterized as a job center with a full accompaniment of retail and entertainment establishments. It has usually developed an identity of its own distinct from the central city with which it is associated, even in the absence of formal jurisdictional boundaries. No mayor or city council governs the SEC, as it is usually part of a larger political jurisdiction. Some SECs that have developed around the country include the Schaumburg area of Chicago, the Perimeter Center area of Atlanta, the Mid-Wilshire/Miracle Mile area in Los Angeles, and the Alewife T Station/North Cambridge area in Boston.

The driving force behind the evolution of the SEC is employment. Employment growth in the suburbs is a direct result of employers' economic decisions specifically designed to reduce costs and penetrate new markets. An employer's economic decision to move to a suburban area is a relatively easy one, considering the lower costs of land, taxes, and labor, more space, newer buildings, reduced crime, parking, and proximity to workers and consumer markets typically found in suburban areas. A study on suburban growth according to industry sector indicates that employment growth occurs in those areas "that offer the best mix of accessibility, lower costs, and land availability."[1] It notes, by example, that technological advances in medicine have permitted doctors to set up outpatient facilities in the suburbs closer to their patients, and that, with the graying of the country, lower land costs enable nursing care facilities to be built less expensively in the suburbs.

The suburbanization of the U.S. workforce has been happening by leaps and bounds since World War II, although many researchers contend that it has been occurring for most of the 20th century. A look at employment growth of recent decades shows surprising results. Key findings of a report on national commuting patterns and trends indicate that over 86 percent of national population growth since 1950 occurred in suburban areas, a relatively consistent pattern throughout the nation. It also notes that about two-thirds of all job increases in metropolitan areas between 1960 and 1980 occurred in suburban areas—meaning that suburban jobs rose from about a third of all metropolitan jobs to almost half.[2] A more recent review of 1990 census data reveals similar demographic shifts toward suburban areas: the number of workers in the United States increased by 78 percent between 1960 and 1990 (twice as fast as the population as a whole, at 39 percent), and those workers are increasingly employed in suburban areas. In the 35 major metropolitan areas in the country, five of every six jobs created since 1960 have been created in the suburbs. Further, jobs in suburban areas of major metropolitan areas increased 159 percent between 1960 and 1990.[3]

While the prevalence of SECs became most notable during the 1970s and the 1980s, research has focused on the subject dating back to the 1950s, when the post–World War II era watched U.S. families move from the city to the suburbs outside the city. The appeal of lower land prices, less congestion and overcrowding, reduced crime, lower taxes, better schools and roads, and a better overall quality of life made the choice easy for many households.

Those who could afford to do so moved to the suburbs in pursuit of the American Dream—owning a single-family, detached house. Frank Lloyd Wright's vision for the suburban landscape was embodied in his Broadacre City, which included no less than one acre for each man, woman, and child.

Characteristics of The Suburban Employment Center

What do Walnut Creek, California, the City Centre area of Southfield, Michigan, the Galleria area of Dallas, Texas, and the South Coast Town Center in Orange County, California, have in common? First, they are only four of nearly 200 suburban employment centers that have developed in the United States over the past 30 years. They also share special characteristics with other SECs that set them apart from older and more traditional cities and towns. *Washington Post* writer Joel Garreau has written extensively on the subject over recent years. Though he uses the term "edge city," Garreau notes how practically every researcher of the subject has coined a different name for this concept in urban development. "Their list of titles by now has become marvelous, rich, diverse, and sometimes unpronounceable. The litany includes urban villages, technoburbs, suburban downtowns, suburban activity centers, major diversified centers, urban cores, galactic cit[ies], pepperoni-pizza cities, [cities] of realms, superbia[s], disurb[s], service cities, perimeter cities, and even peripheral centers."[4]

The concept remains the same, however: a job center that has developed over recent decades outside the central downtown business core of a major city. These job centers are usually found on an interstate highway, near an airport, or sometimes near a university or major research facility.[5] But they also share other characteristics. Garreau identifies five criteria that have been used to classify nearly 200 edge cities.

▼ *Office Space.* With employment a driving force, the SEC must have at least 5 million square feet of leasable office space—an area larger than downtown Wilmington, Delaware.

▼ *Retail Space.* Garreau's edge city must have at least 600,000 square feet of retail space, the equivalent of a fair-sized mall with three anchor stores and anywhere from 80 to 100 specialty shops.

▼ *Workers.* Garreau's edge city has a higher population of workers than it does residents. While the population of bedroom communities decreases on weekday mornings as residents commute to work, the population of an edge city *increases* at 9:00 A.M. as people arrive at work.

▼ *Identity.* The edge city has developed an identity of its own and created for itself a sense of place. The public perceives it as a destination point with a mixture of work, retail, and entertainment offerings.

▼ *Transformation.* An edge city is one that has been transformed from something equivalent to a bedroom community, farmland, or open space to a more urban form within a short period of time. They look nothing like cities of 30 years ago.[6]

Workers in SECs characteristically are employed in white-collar and service jobs, and SECs have no formal political governments with mayors or city councils. A study on large-scale suburban activity centers generally concurs with Garreau's criteria—5 million square feet of office space, 600,000 square feet of retail space, more employees than residents, and a mixture of office and retail uses with some residential and hotel uses—but adds location (within five to 20 miles of a regional central business district) and a different time frame (the majority of development within the past ten years, compared to Garreau's 30-year benchmark).[7]

The concept of SECs remains the same, despite slight variations in the criteria defining them: an urban form of development based on a concentration of employment that offers a variety of additional retail and entertainment uses as well as some housing. The rest of this chapter explores the role that housing can play in maintaining healthy growth and development for both the SEC and the local and regional economies.

The Evolution of The Suburban Employment Center

The concept of the SEC is such a new phenomenon, relative to the evolution of cities over many centuries, that it is useful to inquire not only *how* the SEC developed, but also *why* it developed in recent decades and not long before. To address these issues requires a look at a basic motivating force behind residents' and employers' locational decisions: the preference for working closer to home. If given a choice, a worker is more likely to choose a shorter commute over a longer one, all other factors being equal. The evolution of today's SECs has been largely influenced by the development of economic incentives to fulfill this desire to work closer to home, including improved mobility resulting from improved transportation systems and fuel efficiency and improved communications technology. Fax machines, computers, voice mail, electronic mail, paging systems, and cellular telephones have made it easier to conduct business from locations outside the central city. "Expressways and state-of-the-art technology . . . are behind this decentralization of the urban landscape, as is the collective urge to downsize and meet [employees'] needs."[8]

Garreau identifies four distinct stages in the evolution of an edge city. The first stage is marked by the influx of households to suburban areas. Households moved beyond the city limits in pursuit of an improved lifestyle that afforded them the space, conveniences, and amenities the city could not. Improvements in transportation, such as gasoline-efficient vehicles, public transportation systems, and improved road access, helped to reduce the *effective* distances between suburban areas and the urban core by making it easier (faster and less expensive) to get back and forth.

With significant numbers of households firmly implanted in the suburban landscape, the second stage in the evolution of the SEC takes hold: the emergence of supporting retail services. Retail opportunities develop as a means of addressing the service needs of the growing residential population in the suburbs. People evaluating the prospect of moving to a more remote, suburban location find the nearby convenience of a local pharmacy, dry cleaner, watch repair shop, hardware store, and professional offices of doctors, dentists, lawyers, and accountants appealing. With a new consumer market to capitalize on, these supporting retail services quickly follow, catering to residents' convenience by eliminating the necessity for trips into town.

The establishment of these retail support services attracts even more residents to the suburbs, reinforcing the shift in population to the suburbs. And the increased population in suburban areas creates a potential labor pool from which to draw workers, in turn creating the third wave of SECs' development: the luring of employers to suburban areas by lower land prices, lower taxes, available parking, and the abundant workforce that is now residing in the suburbs and eagerly awaiting an opportunity to work closer to home. With the appeal of employment opportunities nearby, even more households are likely to be lured away from the central city.

Having reached a stage of significant suburban employment with a resident population nearby, the SEC might then be able to support significant educational and cultural facilities. Stage four in the evolution of an edge city, "the era of retrofit," brings "'civilization' to this new frontier."[9] The four case studies later in this book provide examples of a clear progression to this stage of development.

The SEC has emerged as a distinct pattern of real estate development over recent decades. Although evidence supports the continued existence of older, traditional central cities, this new urban form shows no signs of disappearing, and much can be learned about the specific components that make for an economically and environmentally healthy form of human settlement. Housing is one of those components.

Housing Supply and Demand in SECs

Occurring at a time when innovations in communications technology and regional transportation systems were firmly taking hold, the development of the job center was largely predictable, given the attractiveness of lower land costs, lower taxes, more space, and lower crime rates. The forces affecting the availability of *housing* within the SEC have not been quite as predictable, however. The case studies profiled in the next four chapters of this book detail specific public policy initiatives that either encourage or constrain the supply of housing in an SEC.

The government policies enacted in a jurisdiction to direct the development of land are largely a function of public sentiment about how land should be developed.

Subjective by its very nature, public sentiment reflects a community's philosophies, goals, and ideals, particularly with respect to economic growth and prosperity, physical development of the built environment, and demographic shifts with regard to income, racial, and religious inclusivity versus exclusivity. These personal attitudes, goals, and ideals set the stage for public policies that affect specific land use issues, such as the development of housing in an SEC.

If, for example, a community like Walnut Creek views itself as rather exclusive, then the public policies it enacts governing the development of land are expected to reflect, implicitly or explicitly, its unified ideal. Consequently, Walnut Creek's restrictive housing development policies have succeeded in keeping land values, and thus housing prices, very high. If, however, a community realizes the overall regional economic and environmental importance of supporting a wider variety of income levels with a more compact form of development, it would more likely implement public policies with vastly different outcomes. The Southfield, Michigan, case study provides such an example, for Southfield recognized the long-range benefits of planning for a wide array of housing choices as far back as the 1950s. The following subsections explore the effects of more restrictive policies toward housing development in an SEC.

Public Policies and the Availability of Land

Communities in metropolitan areas all over the country have witnessed the detrimental effects of uncontrolled growth, particularly in increasingly congested streets and highways and the strain caused by overburdened public facilities and services without the revenue to support them. Because the costs to support such public infrastructure and services increasingly were shifting to taxpayers, movements were established to relieve significant portions of that burden by ensuring that all new development, in effect, paid for itself.

That attitude of having development pay for itself did not bode well for residential construction in the SEC, however. Because commercial properties generate higher tax revenues for local governments while demanding fewer government services, developable land is often more likely to be dedicated to commercial rather than residential uses. And as the supply of residential land is constrained, its market value increases to the point where housing options become limited, forcing workers who are employed in the SEC to look outside the SEC for less expensive housing. The economic, traffic, and environmental im-

pacts of such constraints to residential land supply have long-term implications for the SEC's economy that can detract from its overall competitiveness in the long term.

Growth management, a buzzword of the 1980s, arose out of the seemingly uncontrolled growth in suburban areas and onto farmland and open spaces. In response to public concern about sprawl and the persistent overburdening of infrastructure and public services, growth management techniques like large-lot zoning and development impact fees were employed to slow and/or control the progression of development into outlying areas.

Unfortunately, well-intentioned public policy initiatives often have unanticipated results. Large-lot zoning has been found to create the exact opposite of the desired effect. Larger lots mean either that more land is needed to accommodate residents, forcing residential development to creep out into the outlying rural areas and encouraging the greater use of cars, or that the restricted supply of residential land increases its value, allowing only higher-priced houses to be built there, excluding a large segment of workers who cannot afford to live near the SEC, and again encouraging the use of cars. Development impact fees create additional costs for the developer, who of course passes them on to the consumer. Again, workers who cannot afford these higher prices must look outside the SEC for housing, again requiring the use of automobiles.

Given the constraints on the supply of developable land for residential uses, higher-density housing becomes a viable alternative for providing a range of housing that will, over the long term, ensure the SEC's overall economic and environmental health and well-being. High-density residential development can abet the preservation of farmland and open spaces, promote the provision of public services and infrastructure, and markedly reduce traffic congestion.

The following four case studies demonstrate different approaches to regulating the supply of land for residential use within an SEC. These approaches are based on public policy choices made in response to public sentiment. One message to be distilled from all four case studies is that, while where business is conducted is changing in metropolitan areas across the country, the supply of residential land that would house the workers employed by these businesses is largely a function of local government policies that encourage or discourage further housing development. In simple terms, SECs generally have evolved from the same set of circumstances, but their evolution into very different entities is the result of wide variances in public policy about the direction of future growth.

Bethesda, Maryland, an SEC in the Washington, D.C., metropolitan area, provides an example of how a jurisdiction's public policy shapes the character of that area. Public policy in Montgomery County, where Bethesda is located, supports high-density housing in and around the Bethesda SEC. The county's governing body approved plans that set the stage for development of 1,500 to 2,700 housing units within the next ten to 15 years and the establishment of nearly 19,000 new jobs.[10] Bethesda is a jurisdiction whose public policies encourage high-density housing as a means of establishing the SEC as a living downtown, but for every Bethesda, there are many other SECs whose public policy works to constrain further residential development.

Regulatory Issues and Practices

The supply of land on which to build housing in an SEC is a critical determinant of the housing equation for the SEC. Regrettably, however, land dedicated for residential development is increasingly in short supply, and the zoning laws that regulate the type of use and intensity of development for that land have driven the price of housing in an SEC very high. Housing prices have risen so high, in fact, that many low- and moderate-income workers, who make up a significant portion of the workforce in the SEC, can no longer afford to live in the SEC near their jobs.

Encouraging the construction of higher-density housing, however, would enable housing development costs to be brought more in line with the income of workers in the SEC. Densities of 20 to 30 dwelling units per acre, for example, are cost-effective for many homebuilders. Townhouses, apartments, and condominiums are popular housing products that permit higher densities and, consequently, lower costs. Garden-density and midrise buildings, usually two to four stories, are popular choices.[11] On the other hand, a high-rise building requires the use of reinforced concrete, adding to the cost of building. And consumers in most markets will probably not pay a premium for densities higher than 30 dwelling units per acre.[12]

High-density housing does not always have to *look* like high-density housing. Clever site design and architectural detailing can afford residents the privacy and curb appeal of lower-density housing. Innovative site plans that include zero-lot-line housing, cluster homes, stacked townhouses, coach homes, and courtyard homes provide alternatives to basic linear townhouse developments and apartment buildings.[13] Architectural detailing and building articulation can give attached housing the appearance of detached housing. A study by graduate students at the University of California–Berkeley found

that architectural details like door recesses, building recesses, and bay windows provide architectural interest and the perception of detached housing—the housing product of choice.[14] It is therefore possible to see where local governments can exert greater influence over the development of higher-density housing. By employing stricter design guidelines that include innovative site plans, urban design criteria, and architectural detailing, development at higher densities can be attractive and functional and offered at lower cost than lower-density/larger-lot housing.

Affordable Housing

High housing prices in SECs have the unfortunate effect of forcing workers to search elsewhere for more diverse housing choices, encouraging them back into their cars and onto already congested roads. Having to move farther away from the SEC to find housing has the long-term effect of depleting the SEC of a workforce with a wide range of skills, decreasing the SEC's competitiveness in the regional economy. Thus, the issue of affordable housing is critical in the SEC equation.

Affordable housing is largely a function of regulations and limited land zoned for residential use. Unfortunately, many workers employed in the SEC can no longer afford to live in the SEC, and the issue of affordable housing no longer pertains only to poverty-level and low-income households. It is also a serious issue for the middle class. Some employers have begun to assist their employees to obtain housing in residential areas that would otherwise be out of reach, finding that providing housing assistance is likely to reduce employee turnover, increase productivity, and generate greater satisfaction and company loyalty. Not only are the costs of replacing and retraining workers reduced, but companies can also become more competitive by being able to attract quality workers.[15] Such an investment by the employer creates obvious advantages for the worker: housing options closer to work, decreased commuting times, increased productivity, choices in the mode of transit used, and, thus, decreases in pollution from automobile traffic. Employers also look to receive returns on their investment through improved public relations within their communities. The "presence of employees living in the neighborhood, greater participation in employer-sponsored social events, and the stability provided by a long-term workforce in the community" are advantages to an employer.[16]

These pioneering employers are farsighted enough to recognize that by encouraging their workers to live nearby, they are enhancing their own economic viability and helping to strengthen the regional economy. Developing public policy mechanisms that encourage rather than discourage more compact development that includes high-density housing makes it possible to offer workers a wider range of housing options, improve productivity, reduce traffic congestion, improve the efficiencies with which residents are served by municipal services and infrastructure, improve air quality, and preserve open space.

Who Is the SEC Housing Consumer?

The following four case studies share a common thread: policy choices made by individual communities determine both the supply of residential land and the regulation of that land with regard to intensity of use. But what can be said about the actual consumers of housing in the SEC? What kinds of housing products are in demand in an SEC?

Successful residential development projects in SECs around the country bear similarities with respect to the housing consumer. Generally speaking, the information age in which we are fully entrenched accounts for the predominance of professional and service industries that occupy office space in SECs. Consequently, service workers are the targeted consumers of housing in SECs. They are of all age groups, including empty nesters, and marital status does not seem to be a factor. Singles, couples, and families are all accommodated in the various types of housing offered, from single-family detached houses to townhouses to condominiums and apartments.

The current demand for housing in most SECs is strong and expected to remain so. The share of development in SECs occupied by the office market will decline, but, as it does, opportunities are created for additional retail and residential development. The expansion of retail offerings will in turn attract more residents, thus ensuring continued demand for housing in the SEC.[17]

What housing products do residents of SECs most prefer? To answer that question, it is helpful to look at factors that motivate consumers. While a single-family, detached house is, by and large, the housing product of choice and a significant amount of single-family detached housing does exist in and around SECs, the availability (or unavailability) of land does not always make it cost-effective to build single-family detached houses exclusively. Land zoned for residential use is generally in short supply and expensive, and the effects of such policies make higher-density housing more profitable for builders and thus more affordable for consumers.

While builders' profits are certainly a motivating factor in choosing whether to build high-density or low-density housing, many other benefits are to be gained by including townhouses, condominiums, and apartments among the mix of housing in an SEC. High-density housing permits a more efficient use of land and of other resources like utilities, roads, and other public services, permitting the preservation of open space and recreation areas. Higher densities also tend to increase activity and interaction among pedestrians, encouraging a more urban atmosphere. A living downtown in the SEC—with activity taking place during both day and evening hours—creates synergistic effects that enhance the social and cultural vitality of the SEC.[18] "Housing is a vital ingredient [in] the Edge City formula," says Sam Massell, former mayor of Atlanta and now president of the Buckhead Coalition (Buckhead is an SEC in the Atlanta metropolitan area). "You've got the workforce that cements the economic viability of the commercial core, and with housing you have both the labor itself and the patronage for retail [establishments]."[19]

The Case for Housing

We have learned that the demand for additional housing in SECs exists, that land on which to build housing—while scarce—can be effectively regulated to make affordable housing possible, and that fiscal and public policy tools with which to increase the supply of housing in SECs are available, though complex. Thus, it is possible to provide more housing. This section explores the question of why more housing *should* be provided.

Transportation and Commuting Patterns

Many researchers believe that the historic pattern of our urban settlements has been driven by the modes of transportation available at the time. Thus, the distances between our homes and our marketplaces were only as far as could be traveled within a reasonable amount of time by foot, by horse, or by car. Today, we are firmly entrenched in the age of the superhighway—both literally, with a vast network of freeways crisscrossing the nation, and figuratively, with the burgeoning advancements in computer and communications technology. We are able to travel great distances by auto, train, plane, and now computer. Our locational choices for setting up a household and supporting that household with income have been liberated to the extent that we are able to work, live, and play at greater distances than ever before.

The consequences of such freedoms have been tendencies toward suburban sprawl, which can be extremely costly, even staggering, to a jurisdiction to provide infrastructure and other public services. A study by the Center for Urban Studies at Rutgers University indicates that the costs of sprawl development over 20 years reached over $1.5 billion, which, when capitalized at current borrowing rates, can reach a total cost of $7 billion to $8 billion.[20] These costs are then passed on to consumers, often in the form of higher housing prices.

Suburban sprawl creates an additional burden on transportation systems as traffic patterns begin to conflict. Neighborhood errands must be made by car as public transportation systems are not financially feasible in remote, sparsely populated locations. Errand traffic then combines with commuter traffic, which is then channeled onto increasingly clogged highways approaching, or exceeding, their carrying capacities.

Thus, the most obvious justification for increasing the amount of housing in SECs is the reduction in automobile traffic. With more compact development and high-density housing closer to work, employees would be more likely to walk to work or use public transportation. "Where workers reside near their work sites, say within two miles, both transit and walking tend to be viable . . . alternatives in suburbia and perhaps are substituted for one another."[21]

An interesting concept integrally related to the advantages of reducing traffic is one in which providing high-density housing seems to create opportunities for even more housing. A study prepared by the planning body for Montgomery and Prince Georges Counties, outside Washington, D.C., explores the idea that by significantly reducing the use of cars, land that was formerly used for surface parking can be put to a more important use—namely, housing. Techniques to reduce the number of trips have proven effective, even by as much as 40 percent, thereby reducing the need for parking. The study provides an analysis of a typical office development in Montgomery County, where, with proper parking reduction management techniques, approximately 22 percent of the site could be made available for enough high-density housing to support 124 dwelling units in an 11-story multifamily building.[22]

Environmental Benefits

Another argument for providing higher-density housing in SECs pertains specifically to environmental quality. The intelligent use of our natural resources can result in improved air quality, more efficient use of infrastructure and public facilities, and conservation of natural green spaces in an urbanized suburban center. To do so requires forethought, creative planning, and effective implementation.

Air quality can easily be improved through the provision of more housing in an SEC, because more housing reduces dependency on the automobile for trips related to household errands, commuting to work, shopping, leisure activities, and entertainment. Another environmental benefit of high-density housing relates to the provision of open space as an integral component of a healthy and well-planned development. Open space is "a valued commodity for urban residents. It provides natural scenery to relieve minds oppressed by dense urban environments. It offers opportunities for many kinds of recreation . . . [and] it contains important ecological resources, such as wetlands, animal and plant habitats, and watersheds, that help maintain air and water quality for everyone."[23]

Compact high-density housing close to employment means that open spaces can be more easily preserved. Even within the SEC's core, clustered buildings and clever site design can create urban parks and jogging/bicycle paths that contribute to workers' and residents' recreational and leisure options.

Choices Affecting Lifestyle

What makes an SEC tick? The same thing that makes traditional city centers vibrant and alive: people. The mixture of all kinds of people—different races, ages, genders, and income levels—creates the vitality and excitement that all urban centers aspire to. And to attract people, choices in housing must be available to them. Too often, choices are not available, and housing prices quickly escalate beyond affordability in many SECs around the country. But only with the provision of sufficient affordable housing will SECs thrive into the next century.

The SEC is a magnet for people for economic reasons. People look to the SEC to provide jobs and an inviting place to shop and spend leisure time. A variety of higher-density housing makes it possible to attract people. Townhouses, for example, are typically found toward the edges of the SEC; as an option for those who cannot yet afford a single-family detached house, they are good choices for young families. Closer to the core of the SEC, apartment dwellers and condominium owners who value proximity to work are more likely to be found. Single adults, couples, and empty nesters often find this type of housing suitable to their lifestyles.

As the country's population ages, an address in the SEC might prove to be even more desirable, as living in an apartment or condominium alleviates the responsibilities for care and maintenance of owning a single-family detached house, whose lawns must be mowed, snow shoveled, and gutters cleaned out. Older citizens can be encouraged to stay physically active by walking to shopping and entertainment.

Finally, increased housing in the SEC promotes the concept of a "living" downtown. With housing interspersed throughout the SEC, activity will occur both day and night. Such an atmosphere creates opportunities for spontaneity. "Having to drive to every destination and appointment precludes the variety of incidents and the potential for casual contact that traditionally made downtown districts good business locations: the ability to set up a meeting on short notice, the chance to run into someone you know at lunch. . . . "[24]

Economic Competitiveness

Industries of all kinds rely increasingly on the advanced technology of computers and telecommunications. While the technology itself enables businesses to operate at greater distances from the central city, their white-collar employees who work with the technology daily are *not* able to live within reasonable commuting distances of their jobs. The long-term effects of it can be quite significant.

Without an adequate supply of housing in the SEC, low- and moderate-income workers must look elsewhere for affordable housing, sometimes necessitating a change in jobs. The costs to employers of attracting and training new workers can be significant. The problems associated with a diminishing pool of workers are serious, so much so that initiatives have been launched to assist residents in their commutes from other areas, usually from the inner city, to the SEC. Such programs, referred to as "reverse commute programs," have been attempted in many metropolitan areas, including Detroit, where inner-city residents were assisted with transportation to jobs in suburban, job-rich areas. Robert Cervero, professor of city and regional planning at the University of California–Berkeley, believes the subsequent failure of Detroit's program was largely because such efforts are only a band-aid solution to a larger, more pervasive problem. "The whole concept [is] fatally flawed[,] . . . [overestimating] the willingness of people to commute long distances to unfamiliar areas where they are not comfortable and to do so for low-paying jobs that do not offer a lot of opportunity. . . . They don't get at the deepest roots of the problem—the lack of housing for the poor in job-rich suburbs. . . . "[25]

Only through the encouragement of high-density housing will workers of a variety of wage levels be able to help maintain the economic competitiveness of their employers and thus the region. "Without an adequate supply of affordable housing for key employees, many companies experience labor shortages that affect their ability to remain competitive in the marketplace. . . . Over time, a decline in the quality of the labor force and shortages of workers at various skill levels are bound to hurt a region's economy."[26]

Two of the following case studies hypothesize that, as housing prices rise, encouraging people to move farther and farther away from their places of employment, a point is reached where traffic congestion and time spent commuting become so unbearable that it becomes viable to pay a higher price for housing closer to employment. The implications of this seemingly reasonable hypothesis could be detrimental to the economy. If it is true that people would be willing to spend a higher percentage of their disposable incomes on housing, then it would follow that a smaller percentage of that disposable income is left over for savings and for purchasing consumer goods. Decreased rates of savings create inflationary pressures, and a prolonged state of reduced consumer spending can slow economic growth. Thus, very real economic reasons exist for attending to shortages in the supply of housing in SECs. "The shortage of accessible, affordable housing is one of the great brakes on how much economic development can occur in a region."[27] The economic health of both the SEC and the larger region depend on action in this arena.

Conclusion

One of the greatest challenges in studying the urban environment is understanding what makes an urban center an inviting place to live, work, and play. The pieces of this puzzle do not work in isolation: each activity contributes to the health and well-being of others. And each person is also a part of something far greater than him- or herself. Much more must be done to recognize the importance of incorporating workers into the permanent fabric of the SEC, for it cannot exist without workers. Businesses cannot run efficiently and profitably with shortages of labor and increased labor costs. It is therefore incumbent upon governing officials to ensure an adequate supply of housing for workers. Suburban employment centers offer an important opportunity to achieve that goal.

Notes

1. Sammis B. White, Lisa S Binkley, and Jeffrey D. Osterman, "The Sources of Suburban Growth," *Journal of the American Planning Association* (Spring 1993): 203.

2. Alan E. Pisarski, *Commuting in America: A National Report on Commuting Patterns and Trends* (Westport, Conn.: Eno Foundation for Transportation, 1987), p. 25.

3. Richard L. Forstall, "Going to Town," *American Demographics* (May 1993): 42–47.

4. Joel Garreau, *Edge City: Life on the New Frontier* (New York: Doubleday, 1991), p. 5.

5. David Birch, "The Market for Industrial and Office Space in America: Projections for the 1990s," *Site Selection* (February 1991): 11.

6. Garreau, *Edge City*, pp. 6–7.

7. Transportation Research Board, "Travel Characteristics of Large-Scale Suburban Activity Centers," *National Cooperative Highway Research Program Report 323* (Washington, D.C.: National Research Council, 1989), p. 10.

8. Susannah Bryan, "Headquarters on the Edge," *Plants Sites and Parks* (January/February 1993): 109–12.

9. Joel Garreau, "Myths about Edge Cities," *Edge City News* (July/August 1992): 2.

10. Gregg Zoroya, "A County's Blueprint for a Bethesda in Boom," *Washington Post*, July 11, 1994; and interview with Don Downing, community planner, Maryland–National Capital Park and Planning Commission, Silver Spring, Maryland, September 26, 1994.

11. Christopher Leinberger, Robert Charles Lesser & Co., and Ron Witten, M/PF Research, Inc., cited in Burke Davis III, "Get a Life: Bringing It All Home in Edge City," *Edge City News* (April 1994): 2.

12. Ibid.

13. These configurations and others are described in James W. Wentling and Lloyd W. Bookout, eds., *Density by Design* (Washington, D.C.: ULI–the Urban Land Institute, 1988).

14. Ruth Eckdish Knack, "The One-Acre Habit Is Hard to Break," *Planning* (August 1991): 11.

15. Thomas Deyo, "Employer-Assisted Housing: Strategies for Revitalizing Communities," *Journal of Housing* (September/October 1991): 227–36.

16. Ibid., p. 235.

17. Leinberger and Witten, cited in Davis, "Get a Life," p. 1.

18. The individual case studies provide specific examples of high-density housing that works well in each respective region. They also provide insight as to additional motivating forces that distinguish consumers' tastes and preferences.

19. Davis, "Get a Life," p. 2.

20. Kevin Kasowski, "The Costs of Sprawl, Revisited," *PAS Memo* (Chicago: American Planning Association, February 1993): 1.

21. Robert Cervero, "Land Uses and Travel at Suburban Activity Centers," *Transportation Quarterly* (October 1991): 486.

22. Patrick H. Hare, Larry Ponsford, Joe Davis, Caroline Honig, and Megan Carroll, "Trip Reduction and Affordable Housing: Using Growth Management to Make Housing More Affordable," Staff Report (Silver Spring: Maryland–National Capital Park and Planning Commission). Presented by COMSIS of Silver Spring, Maryland, at the 1991 Transportation Research Board 70th Annual Meeting, January 13–17, 1991, Washington, D.C.

23. Douglas R. Porter, *About Growth Management: Defining the Issues, Assessing the Techniques*, Monograph 110 (Arlington, Va.: NAIOP, 1992), p. 25.

24. Johnathan Barnett, "Accidental Cities: The Deadly Grip of Outmoded Zoning," *Architectural Record* (February 1992): 96.

25. Penelope Lemov, "The Impossible Commute," *Governing* (June 1993): 33.

26. Michael P. Curzan and Amanda Carney, "Lack of Affordable Housing Spurs Employer-Supported Housing Programs," *Urban Land* (July 1989): 6.

27. David A. Heenan, "From Suburbia to Penturbia: Corporate America Goes over the Edge," *Plants Sites and Parks* (January/February 1993): 113–15.

Chapter 2
▲▲▲▲▲▲▲▲▲▲

Walnut Creek, California

by
Nina J. Gruen

Gruen Gruen + Associates
San Francisco, California

*The case study of Walnut Creek was
completed in August 1993.*

Organization of the Case Study

Downtown Walnut Creek, located in rapidly growing Contra Costa County, California, was selected as one of the four employment centers for several reasons: 1) its rapid employment growth and central location within one of the fastest-growing counties in northern California; 2) its highly concentrated downtown commercial area, located directly on the BART line; 3) its poor highway accessibility, stemming from the fact that the freeways and BART run along the western border of the city and houses are spread out to the east; 4) its limited supply of land for future residential development; and 5) a growing antigrowth sentiment, as evidenced by voter-supported bans and restrictions on building that grew in intensity during the 1980s.

It is difficult to evaluate Walnut Creek's present relationship of housing, employment, and commute times without an understanding of the key demographic, employment, real estate development, and retail sales tax shifts that have occurred over time. This historic perspective is presented in the next section.

The third section focuses on the restraints on housing development and their effect on the mix of housing products and prices in and around Walnut Creek. It discusses the way in which attitudes toward growth affect housing development, particularly high-density and affordable housing. Paradoxically, while increased traffic congestion is the reason given to restrict the amount of residential development, this limitation in the housing supply serves to increase the total number of vehicle-miles traveled. The section traces Walnut Creek's land use policies from the early 1970s, showing a tightening of the amount of housing permitted at buildout. Finally, the section shows the relationship between city policy and development in the downtown core. It also presents the economics of developing high-density residential housing in the core area that results from high land values and cost-raising regulations, such as the requirement for street-level commercial space.

The fourth section explores the effect of the mismatch between the expansion of economic activity and the residential base of Walnut Creek and the surrounding communities. It analyzes the shifts in where residents and workers live that accompanied the intensification of commercial activities in the core.

The shorter- and longer-term impacts of the decisions and actions taken by the city of Walnut Creek are summarized in the final section. It discusses the ways in which past and present land use policies have resulted in a constriction of available land designated for residential use. These policies and actions make it unlikely that significant amounts of high-density housing will be added in or near the downtown unless public redevelopment is invoked. Public redevelopment would be required, because most land designated for higher-density residential use is currently occupied by older low-density residential and commercial uses.

The Metamorphosis Of an Edge City

Walnut Creek incorporated as a city in 1914 but did not begin its urban/suburban life until after World War II. By 1950, the city housed only 2,420 residents, many of whom were employed as pickers and cultivators of walnut trees. Formerly named Crossroads, Walnut Creek is located at the crossroads of central Contra Costa County. In the 1950s, a freeway system was built through Walnut Creek that reinforced Crossroads's function, even though by that time the name was no longer applied. But the freeway was not designed to accommodate rapid growth within Walnut Creek, and initially it served mainly to allow Contra Costa County residents to travel to center cities like Oakland and San Francisco and some smaller cities like Berkeley for work and shopping.

Walnut Creek's population increased to 10,000 by 1960, to 40,000 by 1970, to 53,600 by 1980, and to 60,569 by 1990. In the recessionary period from 1990 to 1992, Walnut Creek attracted another 1,500 residents. The 1990 Census also shows that almost 80 percent of the city's housing stock was built between 1950 and 1990.

The history of Walnut Creek since 1960 fits almost perfectly the four growth stages of suburban activity centers described in Joel Garreau's *Edge Cities*. In 1990, Walnut Creek reached the fourth stage when the $20 million Regional Center for the Arts opened its doors. The arts center, which includes two theaters and an art gallery and provides a host of musical and theatrical programs, currently draws 250,000 visitors per year. As anticipated, this downtown center has, in turn, attracted additional restaurants, bookstores, and a movie complex, making downtown Walnut Creek a more interesting place to be.

The population growth that has continued to move Walnut Creek through the early stages of the metamorphosis to an activity center or edge city has been caused by more than the city's functioning as a bedroom community and then as a job site. Walnut Creek has also long served as a magnet for older retirees, with one of the oldest and largest retirement communities in northern Cali-

▼ ▼

Figure 2-1
Commercial Building Activity in Walnut Creek (January 1, 1975, to September 30, 1992)

	Square Feet	Average per Year
Total Retail	272,300	15,341
Nonoffice Other than Retail	704,780	39,706
Office	5,446,964	306,871
Total*	6,424,044	

*These figures do not take into account floor area torn down, filled in, or destroyed or Measure H–exempted projects. Measure H projects include hospitals and other institutions like nursing homes, churches, schools, and daycare facilities.
Source: City of Walnut Creek.

▲ ▲

fornia, the 8,500-person community of Rossmoor. The average age of Rossmoor residents is 77. In fact, one-third of the city's population is over the age of 55, according to the 1990 Census.

The Emergence of Walnut Creek as a Major Economic Activity Center

While population growth was an early spur to the change from a rural crossroads to a prototypical 1990s activity center, the big and final engine of change was the growth of the city's employment base. In 1980, the city had 37,345 jobs. Between 1980 and 1990, the decade when BART reached Walnut Creek, employment increased further. This case study concentrates on this period in its discussion of the relationship among jobs, housing, and commuting.

The land use base for the expansion of employment started its expansion in the mid-1970s. Between 1975, by which time a sizable retail base already existed, and 1985, approximately 6.3 million gross square feet of commercial space was built in Walnut Creek. Between 100,000 and 200,000 square feet of additional space was added after 1985. Figure 2-1 presents an estimate of the commercial space added in Walnut Creek between 1974 and September 1992.[1]

Figure 2-2 presents the changes in employment within the city of Walnut Creek's sphere of influence for 1980 and 1990. All sectors, with the exception of agriculture

Figure 2-2
Employment in Walnut Creek (1980 and 1990)*

	1980	1990	Net Change	Percent Change
Agriculture and Mining	680	550	−130	−19.1
Manufacturing and Wholesale	3,942	5,440	1,498	38.0
Retail	8,180	11,650	3,470	42.4
Service	13,086	19,640	6,554	50.1
Other Employment	11,457	16,220	4,763	41.6
Total	37,345	53,500	16,155	43.3

*Employment estimates are for Walnut Creek's sphere of influence.
Sources: Association of Bay Area Governments, *Projections '92, Recession Update*; Gruen Gruen – Associates.

▲ ▲

and mining, experienced an increase in employment, with the largest increase in both numbers and percentages in the service sector. The service sector added 6,554 jobs, for a net increase of 50.1 percent. In Walnut Creek between 1980 and 1990, 16,155 net total jobs were added.

A more refined breakdown of private-sector employment by Walnut Creek zip codes for 1981 and 1991 is presented in Figure 2-3. The zip codes are not directly

coterminous with the city's sphere of influence (see Figure 2-4). The CBD is in zip code 94596. Between 1981 and 1991, this zip code experienced an increase of 14,209 jobs. Increases in employment in Transportation, Communication, and Utilities (TCU) (3,323), Finance/ Insurance/Real Estate (FIRE) (5,438), and Services (10,349) account for nearly 90 percent of the 22,157 total job increase between 1981 and 1991. The 94596 zip code accounted for 11,459, or 60 percent, of the 19,110 net additions in jobs from 1981 to 1991 in the three fastest-growing sectors.

Retail Sales

Walnut Creek has not only become a major job base, but also grown to house a major retailing center. Figure 2-5 shows the retail sales experienced (in constant 1992 dollars) for Walnut Creek for 1970 through 1992, by major category. The last three columns show the percentage change for 1970 to 1992, 1980 to 1992, and 1990 to 1992. Between 1970 and 1992, when Walnut Creek experienced a 104 percent increase in constant dollar sales, the state saw sales increase by 69 percent, the county by 96 percent.

The city experienced actual percentage increases in all categories except liquor stores (which have decreased in sales nationally), drugstores, grocery stores, building materials and farm implements, and service stations between 1980 and 1992. More significant, the city experienced major increases in sales in general merchandise

▼ ▼

Figure 2-3
Private-Sector Employment by Zip Codes in Walnut Creek (1981 and 1991)

	1981					1991					Percent Change, 1981–1991
	Zip Code 94595	Zip Code 94596	Zip Code 94598	Zip Code Total	Percent	Zip Code 94595	Zip Code 94596	Zip Code 94598	Zip Code Total	Percent	
Agriculture	77	128	10	215	0.7	51	209	67	327	0.6	52.1
Mining and Construction	114	880	162	1,156	3.8	199	1,057	275	1,531	2.9	32.4
Manufacturing	14	2,338	1,390	3,742	12.2	23	1,287	1,687	2,997	5.7	−19.9
TCU	8	1,301	411	1,720	5.6	77	4,137	829	5,043	9.5	193.2
Wholesale	35	1,036	238	1,309	4.3	61	1,053	341	1,455	2.7	11.2
Retail	210	5,228	2,736	8,174	26.7	413	8,754	2,166	11,333	21.5	38.6
FIRE	417	2,801	1,414	4,632	15.1	419	6,063	3,588	10,070	19.1	117.4
Services	613	5,974	3,116	9,703	31.6	1,320	11,335	7,397	20,052	38.0	106.7
Total	1,488	19,686	9,477	30,651	100.0	2,563	33,895	16,350	52,808	100.0	72.3

Sources: Association of Bay Area Governments; Gruen Gruen + Associates.

▲ ▲

Figure 2-4
Location of Zip Codes within the City of Walnut Creek

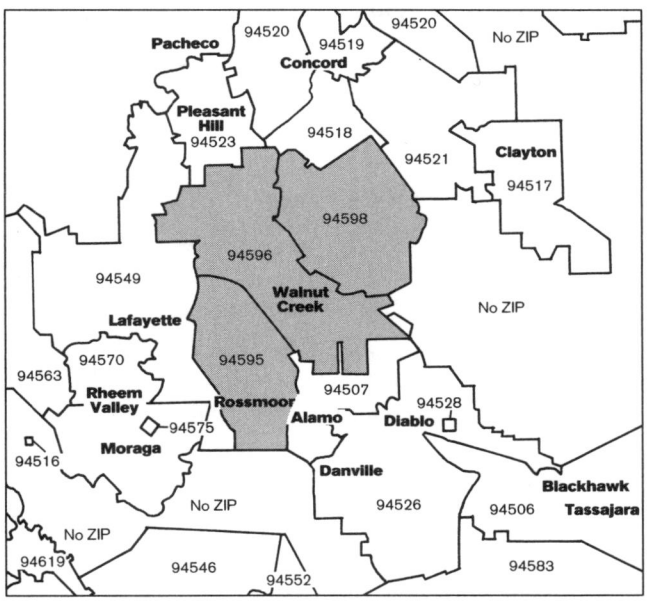

(42 percent), apparel (22 percent), restaurants and bars (27 percent), home furnishings and appliances (21 percent), auto dealers and supplies (39 percent), and other retail stores (90 percent). Figure 2-6 shows the per capita retail sales for Walnut Creek, also in constant dollars, and Figure 2-7 shows the same data for the county.

In 1980, per capita sales for all retail goods totaled $12,358 for the city of Walnut Creek and $8,500 for Contra Costa County (1992 dollars). By 1990, per capita sales in Walnut Creek had increased to $15,052, while sales in the county had decreased to $7,091. Between 1990 and 1992, Walnut Creek lost some per capita sales revenues as a result of the recession. Per capita sales decreased to $12,811, while the county's decreased to $6,404. Thus, even in a recessionary period, Walnut Creek's per capita sales remained twice that of the county, confirming the designation of Walnut Creek as an important activity center within Contra Costa County. These high per capita sales figures reflect the ability of stores in Walnut Creek to serve the residents of the county. Because retail sales in Walnut Creek's full range of stores do include many dollars spent by people who do not live in Walnut Creek, per capita sales in Walnut Creek are able to grow much faster than sales in this prosperous and expanding county.

Figure 2-5
Retail Sales in Constant 1992 Dollars for Walnut Creek

Category	1970 ($000)	1975 ($000)	1980 ($000)	1985 ($000)	1990 ($000)	1992 ($000)	Percent Change, 1970–1992	Percent Change, 1980–1992	Percent Change, 1990–1992
Apparel Stores	41,677	41,542	53,758	55,434	68,500	65,700	57.64	22.21	−4.09
General Merchandise Stores	65,138	102,999	93,899	125,120	152,709	133,800	105.41	42.49	−12.38
Drugstores	22,706	20,987	27,109	25,768	25,288	25,700	13.19	−5.20	1.63
Grocery Stores	44,942	64,849	61,436	74,915	35,963	41,600	−7.44	−32.29	15.67
Liquor Stores	9,692	10,140	8,220	2,737	0	0	–	–	–
Restaurants and Bars	36,683	52,222	63,834	67,356	81,234	81,000	120.81	26.89	−0.29
Home Furnishings and Appliances	22,241	20,357	23,684	29,040	25,655	28,700	29.04	21.18	11.87
Building Materials/ Farm Implements	8,353	14,561	51,460	53,570	52,467	43,000	414.78	−16.44	−18.04
Auto Dealers and Supplies	92,920	111,420	138,042	234,622	235,184	192,700	107.38	39.59	−18.06
Service Stations	3,923	46,530	72,071	59,149	50,439	39,000	894.14	−45.89	−22.68
Other Retail Stores	40,270	60,408	75,061	111,418	182,068	142,600	254.11	89.98	−21.68
Total	388,545	546,014	668,575	839,130	909,507	793,800	104.30	18.73	−12.72

Note: Numbers might not add because of rounding.
Sources: California State Board of Equalization, *Taxable Sales in California*; U.S. Bureau of Labor Statistics; California Dept. of Finance, Demographic Research Unit; Gruen Gruen + Associates.

Figure 2-6
Retail Sales per Capita in Constant 1992 Dollars for Walnut Creek

Category	1970	1975	1980	1985	1990	1992
Apparel Stores	$1,045.99	$ 902.11	$ 993.68	$ 987.24	$ 1,133.68	$ 1,060.33
General Merchandise Stores	1,634.83	2,236.68	1,735.66	2,228.28	2,527.33	2,159.39
Drugstores	569.86	455.75	501.08	458.91	418.51	414.77
Grocery Stores	1,127.96	1,408.22	1,135.61	1,334.17	595.18	671.38
Liquor Stores	243.24	220.20	151.95	48.74	0.00	0.00
Restaurants and Bars	920.67	1,134.02	1,179.93	1,199.56	1,344.42	1,307.25
Home Furnishings and Appliances	558.19	442.07	437.79	517.18	424.60	463.19
Building Materials/Farm Implements	209.65	316.20	951.19	954.04	868.33	693.97
Auto Dealers and Supplies	2,332.09	2,419.54	2,551.62	4,178.40	3,892.30	3,109.97
Service Stations	98.47	1,010.42	1,332.17	1,053.40	834.77	629.42
Other Retail Stores	1,010.70	1,311.80	1,387.44	1,984.26	3,013.22	2,301.41
Total	$9,751.66	$11,856.99	$12,358.13	$14,944.18	$15,052.33	$12,811.08
Population*	39,844	46,050	54,100	56,151	60,423	61,962

*1970 estimate is for April 1; 1975 through 1992 estimates are for January 1.
Note: Numbers might not add because of rounding.
Sources: California State Board of Equalization, *Taxable Sales in California*; U.S. Bureau of Labor Statistics; California Dept. of Finance, Demographic Research Unit; Gruen Gruen + Associates.

Figure 2-7
Retail Sales per Capita in Constant 1992 Dollars for Contra Costa County

Category	1970	1975	1980	1985	1990	1992
Apparel Stores	$ 338.66	$ 318.31	$ 338.52	$ 344.94	$ 363.65	$ 341.27
General Merchandise Stores	1,169.24	1,289.06	1,203.72	1,113.92	1,302.66	1,233.76
Drugstores	227.45	229.51	213.28	254.96	226.18	216.28
Grocery Stores	546.42	621.82	574.75	697.34	584.37	594.36
Liquor Stores	170.83	181.89	154.47	80.07	65.82	56.16
Restaurants and Bars	432.31	583.15	647.00	695.13	694.18	667.61
Home Furnishings and Appliances	216.45	247.37	369.97	427.99	358.04	302.79
Building Materials/Farm Implements	231.52	322.76	512.73	492.82	618.93	508.80
Auto Dealers and Supplies	822.09	914.43	886.60	1,280.57	1,076.45	873.61
Service Stations	231.18	1,023.46	2,896.36	917.62	715.20	599.26
Other Retail Stores	438.57	591.71	702.49	1,022.15	1,085.59	1,010.07
Total	$4,824.73	$6,323.49	$8,499.88	$7,327.53	$7,091.07	$6,403.97
Population*	566,116	583,400	651,600	704,619	797,585	836,871

*1970 estimate is for April 1; 1975 through 1992 estimates are for January 1.
Note: Numbers might not add because of rounding.
Sources: California State Board of Equalization, *Taxable Sales in California*; U.S. Bureau of Labor Statistics; California Dept. of Finance, Demographic Research Unit; Gruen Gruen + Associates.

Housing Production and Prices

While the range of jobs and the demographic composition of customers served by Walnut Creek stores and service providers expanded dramatically, the range of housing prices offered did not. Figure 2-8 reviews the average prices and increases in 1980 and 1990 for the seven communities within 6.9 miles of downtown Walnut Creek. Housing in Walnut Creek and its neighboring communities continued to serve only the more affluent households of the region, even as local jobs provided a broader range of incomes and local stores and professionals served a broader range of incomes.

Figure 2-9 indicates that *if* the increase in housing stock in the communities around Walnut Creek had widened, the affordability range offered could have served the households that contained the added jobs provided by the area. That is, if the 31,750 residential units added between 1980 and 1990 had been available to the households of the 50,961 jobholders added to the city's employment base, the strain on the regional transportation network would not have been increased. At the countywide average of 1.7 employed persons per household, the added employment of 50,961 jobs equals about 30,000 households. But even in Concord, the city with the lowest-priced housing within the 6.9-mile radius, the average house price was $193,900 in 1990. As shown on Figure 2-8, with the exception of Pleasant Hill and Concord, the communities around Walnut Creek exceed that city's 1990 median house price of $289,300. At $720 median

gross rent, rental values in Walnut Creek were lower than all but one of the other comparable communities. An average rent of $720 would require a household income of approximately $29,000, under the assumption that the household spends 30 percent of its income to pay for shelter.

If only the two communities in the county that are now activity centers, Concord and Walnut Creek, are evaluated, a major imbalance exists when comparing the net addition of jobs to the net addition of households between 1980 and 1990. Walnut Creek added 3,387 households and 16,155 jobs, while Concord added 7,444 households and 28,322 jobs. It is this imbalance, combined with the high cost of nearby housing, that has resulted in more extensive commutes over time.

If Walnut Creek had maintained the same ratio of jobs to occupied housing in 1990 that it showed in 1980, it would have had to build an additional 23,000 housing units. In 1980, Walnut Creek had 69,680 occupied dwellings and 37,340 jobs, or a housing-to-jobs ratio of 1.8. By 1990, this ratio had decreased to 1.4 (73,067 ÷ 53,500 = 1.36). If it had maintained a 1.8 ratio in 1990, the number of occupied households would have been approximately 96,000. For the close-in communities, including Walnut Creek, the ratio dropped from 2.7 to 2.0. The failure of Walnut Creek to provide enough additional residential units to house its workforce and the continued escalation of housing prices in Walnut Creek and the adjoining communities are not independent events. Housing prices went up because the policies of Walnut

▼▼▼

Figure 2-8

Increase in Median Gross Rent, Median House Price, per Capita Income, and per Household Income for Walnut Creek and Nearby Communities (1980 and 1990)[1]

Cities	Median Gross Rent			Median House Price			Per Capita Income			Per Household Income		
	1980	1990	Percent Change	1980	1990	Percent Change	1980	1990	Percent Change	1980	1990	Percent Change
Walnut Creek	$337	$ 720	110	$144,341	$289,300	100	$12,684	$26,354	110	$28,781	$ 55,745	90
Pleasant Hill	338	759	120	100,831	228,500	180	9,787	21,950	120	25,035	52,791	110
Concord	319	677	110	96,536	193,900	100	8,887	17,566	100	23,977	46,147	90
Alamo	495	1,001	100	200,213	500,000	150	17,371	43,705	150	53,880	125,841	130
Danville	476	1,001	110	172,408	360,100	110	13,275	31,265	140	41,931	87,399	110
Lafayette	377	767	130	170,057	388,500	130	14,564	34,281	140	38,951	88,764	130
Orinda[2]	–	871	–	–	406,500	–	–	31,122	–	–	87,117	–

[1]Cities are within seven miles of downtown Walnut Creek.
[2]Orinda was not incorporated as a city in 1980.
Sources: Association of Bay Area Governments Regional Data Center; Gruen Gruen + Associates.

▲▲▲

Figure 2-9
Increase in Number of Households and Jobs for Walnut Creek And Nearby Communities (1980 and 1990)[1]

	Households (1980)	Households (1990)	Net Increase in Households (No.)	Net Increase in Households (Percent)	Jobs (1980)	Jobs (1990)	Net Increase in Jobs (No.)	Net Increase in Jobs (Percent)
Walnut Creek[2]	69,680	73,067	3,387	5	37,345	53,500	16,155	40
Pleasant Hill[2]	29,617	37,923	8,306	3	11,631	14,770	3,139	30
Concord[2]	105,167	112,611	7,444	10	34,348	62,670	28,322	80
Alamo/Blackhawk[3]	10,215	18,785	8,570	80	2,621	2,790	169	10
Danville[2]	29,385	31,982	2,597	10	6,785	7,810	1,025	20
Lafayette[2]	23,785	24,829	1,044	4	8,116	9,590	1,474	20
Orinda[2]	16,169	16,573	404	2	3,184	3,860	676	20
Total	284,018	315,770	31,752		104,030	154,990	50,961	

[1]Cities are within seven miles of downtown Walnut Creek.
[2]City sphere of influence.
[3]Urban service area.
Sources: Association of Bay Area Governments, *Projections '92*, July 1992; Gruen Gruen + Associates.

Creek and the communities around it constrained growth and exacted a heavy price in quality, amenities, and other contributions to the community from those builders they allowed to develop. The following section discusses these policies and the manner in which they worked to keep Walnut Creek and, even more so, the cities around it the preserve of relatively well-to-do residents, while providing jobs, goods, and services for workers and consumers with a broad range of incomes.

Restraints on Housing Development and Their Effect on the Product and Price Mix of Housing in And around Walnut Creek

Perhaps because of the growth that occurred in Walnut Creek and nearby communities, a growing sentiment against new development became evident in the late 1970s. While public policy came to include restraints on commercial as well as residential development, it was and is the former that is more restrictive. Although traffic congestion is the reason given for much of the antigrowth sentiment, including Measure H passed by the voters in

1985, one effect of restraining residential development has been to increase vehicle-miles traveled.

Development Attitudes and Policies in Walnut Creek

Attitudes toward development in Walnut Creek are not uniform. Currently, the city has four political action committees (PACs), each with its own agenda: the Walnut Creek Coalition, Citizens for a Better Walnut Creek, Walpac, and 10,000 Friends of Walnut Creek. It is perhaps the division in the community, as illustrated by the PACs, that has kept Walnut Creek from being even more restrictive than it has been. For example, Measure O on the November 5, 1991, ballot was defeated. Measure O was approved to go on the ballot in July 1991; it was seen as a way to implement a growth-limitation program to replace Measure H, which was overturned by the Supreme Court in 1990. Measure O, Mandatory Growth Limitation and Scenic Open Space Protection Plan Ordinance, would have required the City Council to choose an average annual population growth rate that would not exceed 2 percent for the three-year period. Once every three years, the City Council was also to choose an average annual commercial growth rate that would not exceed 200,000 square feet. Measure O also included the City Council's right to reject or modify projects that increased peak-hour traffic at any affected intersection by more than 2 percent.

In 1991, the voters defeated Measure O, and the city subsequently embarked on a planning process that has resulted in revisions to the 1989 General Plan. According to an article in the July/August 1993 edition of *In A Nutshell*, published by the city of Walnut Creek, "a divided City Council voted to follow most of the Planning Commission's recommended growth limitation plan for Walnut Creek over one proposed by its own Community Character Committee." The Community Character Committee consists of the two City Council members with the strongest no-growth position. The article goes on to say:

> The Commission's plan was viewed as a more flexible version of the Committee's proposal, which called for a 16½-year span and a cap of 900,000 square feet of commercial and retail development. . . . In adopting the Commission's plan, the Council majority favored restricting commercial development to a rate of 150,000 square feet every two years. The Council majority also agreed the maximum size of a project would be no more than 75 percent of a two-year allocation (112,000 square feet in 1993–95). Further, no more than 255 new houses per year could be built.

The Council also rejected the Community Character Committee's rigidly enforced traffic standards and instead indicated a project could be approved if it earned so-called "preference points" for desirable qualities, such as sales tax revenues and an enhanced downtown.

Despite the general reduction in allowable development, the General Plan designated the downtown core area as the location where most future commercial development will be encouraged. The revision of the General Plan, approved July 27, 1993, however, includes a reduction in the height limit and/or density of development—though replacement housing in the core Golden Triangle area was exempted from the roadway service standards that serve as a major impediment to most new high-density development. The height limitation was enacted to bring the General Plan into conformance with Measure A, which had been approved by the voters in 1985.

Unfortunately, from the viewpoint of housing production, dropping residential development to an average of no more than 255 units per year is just one more step in the direction of increasing restraints on residential development. One can get a feel for the manner in which the policy screws on housing development have been constantly tightened by reviewing the history of planned and actual production since 1971. Figure 2-10 compares the estimate of Walnut Creek's 1980 and 1990 housing stock contained in the 1971 General Plan with the actual housing stock on these dates (but note that the data in the 1971 General Plan are for the planning area, while actual stock is for the city of Walnut Creek). According to a Walnut Creek associate planner, about 81 percent of the planning area's stock is located in the city.

▼▼

Figure 2-10
Comparison of Estimated Housing Stock in Walnut Creek in the 1971 General Plan with Actual Housing Stock in Walnut Creek (1980 and 1990)

	Estimated Stock for Planning Area*			Actual Stock within City's Boundaries		
	1980	1990	Estimated Additions to Stock	1980	1990	Net Additions to Stock
Detached Single-Family	17,000	18,000	1,000	12,311	16,024	3,713
Attached Single-Family	2,900	6,200	3,300			
Multifamily	9,300	12,200	2,900	12,094	13,944	1,850
Rossmoor	6,600	10,000	3,400			
Total	35,800	46,400	10,600	24,405	29,968	5,563
Average Annual Addition			1,060			556

*Estimated stock is for the planning area. A Walnut Creek associate planner estimates that approximately 19 percent of this total is located outside the city's jurisdictional boundaries. Therefore, the city's estimated stock was 29,000 in 1980 and 37,600 in 1990, suggesting a net increase of 8,600 units during the 1980s instead of the approximately 5,000 units actually added.

Sources: Association of Bay Area Governments; California Dept. of Finance; City of Walnut Creek 1971 General Plan, Appendix 4; Gruen Gruen + Associates.

▲▲

When the 1971 Plan was done, the planners and those who approved the plan envisioned a city with more housing than is contemplated in more recent plans.[2] Thus, they assumed in 1971 that the city would have a housing stock of 29,000 by 1980 and 37,600 by 1990. Actually, the 1980 stock climbed only to 24,405. Even by 1990, the city's housing stock had climbed to only 29,968 units. Further, the net average annual addition is 65 percent of what had been initially estimated, if one looks only at the net annual additions within the city of Walnut Creek for 1980 to 1990. Only 3,713 single-family units (both attached and detached) and 1,850 multifamily units had been built during the 1980s. (Rossmoor's 2,900 single- and 3,400 multifamily housing units are included in these totals.)

Figure 2-11 is from the 1989 General Plan, Vision 2005, and the estimates shown presume buildout. By 1989, buildout was postulated to be somewhat over 36,000, including the 1,600 units in the pipeline at that time, or approximately 10,000 fewer units than the buildout estimated in 1971. The 1989 General Plan does not envision buildout occurring by 2005. Instead, the report states that over the 17 years of the Plan, 4,600 units would be a more reasonable estimate, or approximately 270 dwellings per year. And, as previously noted, the July 1993 revision to the General Plan limits the average annual addition over the next years to 253 units.

How have these policies affected housing production in the 6.9 miles around downtown Walnut Creek? As discussed earlier, the first half of the 1980s was when Walnut Creek became a major job center with expanded employment, services, and shopping. But the 1980s ushered in only the most minimal broadening of the range of housing prices offered in and near the city. Because housing production was constrained from about 1985 onward, the supply of affordable housing remained tight, and the community now serves primarily households with incomes higher than those who lived in Walnut Creek before it became a major activity center.

As exemplified by what has happened and is happening in the neighboring community of Orinda, Walnut Creek's constraints on residential development were mild when compared to its neighbors. While Walnut Creek's restrictions might appear exceptionally onerous, the truth is that Walnut Creek's policies have historically been more accommodating to future growth than those of nearby communities like Orinda that serve an even higher-income, primarily bedroom population base.

Orinda has been and continues to be an upper-end, low-density residential community. In 1980, the city contained 3,184 jobs and by 1990, 3,420 within the city's borders. Of those who reside in Orinda, 1,018 were employed in the city in 1980, 1,494 in 1990. Thus, despite the fact that total local jobs increased by only 236, the number of locally employed residents increased by almost double that amount, or 476. The city incorporated in July 1985 to control its land use destiny, according to current planning director Irwin Kaplan. Between 1980 and 1990, the city of Orinda and its sphere of influence added a total of 404 to its 1980 stock of 16,169 dwellings, an average of about 40 units per year.

As of January 1990, the city of Orinda (as distinct from its sphere of influence) contained 6,468 dwelling units, 95 percent of them single-family houses on typically half-acre lots.

Multifamily housing consisted of two condominium buildings containing 63 units, 150 senior village units, and Orindawoods, a clustered development consisting of 258 units. The Orindawoods complex has 52 multifamily townhouses, 50 attached units, and 156 single-family detached houses. At the time the 1990 Housing Element was prepared, the least expensive two-bedroom/one-bathroom condominiums were located on Brookwood Road and were priced at about $200,000. Orindawoods's townhouses were listed at a minimum of $340,000 at that time. Houses over $500,000 and $1 million are on the market in substantial numbers.

According to the city's 1990 Housing Element, the Association of Bay Area Governments projected a need for a total of 269 affordable housing units: 43 very-low-, 32 low-, 46 moderate-, and 148 above-moderate-income units. Of that number, 143 was the stated projected need for 1990 to 1995.

▼ ▼

Figure 2-11
Housing in Walnut Creek in the 1989 General Plan, Vision 2005

| | Number of Units | | |
	1988 (Existing)	2005 (Estimated)	Estimated Increase, Assuming Buildout
Single-Family	14,800	16,600	1,800
Multifamily	8,600	11,500	2,900
Rossmoor	5,600	6,900	1,300
Total	29,000	35,100	6,100*
Average Annual Addition			453

*The 6,100 units excludes 1,600 units in the pipeline: 6,100 + 1,600 = 7,700 • 17 years = 453.

Note: Numbers might not add because of rounding.

Source: City of Walnut Creek, 1989 General Plan, Vision 2005, pp. 2–11.

▲ ▲

In cities like Orinda, despite the relatively high-income categories (moderate income in 1990, for example, was defined as households with annual incomes of $35,301 to $52,900), extremely high land costs and related entitlement costs make the provision of multifamily housing, particularly *affordable* multifamily units, extremely difficult to achieve. The city has, however, exempted affordable single-family and multifamily housing from development impact fees, provided the developer signs a written contract with the city restricting the use to affordable housing for 30 years.

The 1990 Housing Element indicates that Orinda had sufficient residential acreage (418 acres) to accommodate 674 additional dwelling units at buildout. Of them, 496 were designated multifamily. Of the 496 designated multifamily units, 400 were designated for the Gateway project.

A May 1993 fiscal impact analysis of the Gateway Valley Specific Plan examines two alternatives. Alternative A indicates a total of 271 units, including 46 12-per-acre and 40 eight-per-acre multifamily units. Alternative B proposes a total of 311 dwellings, with 46 12-per-acre, 32 eight-per-acre, and 41 six-per-acre units, for a total of 119 multifamily units—only 25 percent of the number of units designated in the city's Housing Element.

The 46 12-per-acre units have been designated as affordable and are anticipated to be priced at $190,000. These 46 units are subject to the Specific Plan's requirement to remain affordable for 30 years. The eight-per-acre townhouses are estimated to sell for $425,000, the six-per-acre cottages for $540,000 per dwelling. To receive permission to develop this approximately 1,000-acre Gateway project, the developer has agreed to provide a high level of amenities, including approximately 30 acres of parkland and playfields, an on-site sports/civic complex, and a site for a school. From the outset, the developer has incorporated over 600 acres of open space, an athletic club, an 18-hole golf course, a 260-room conference center/spa, and 50 casitas in his development proposal. Nonetheless, despite the costly mitigations and the lengthy approval process, the implementation of this project is currently being threatened by a prospective citizens' referendum.

The attitudes and policies of Orinda differ little from the other higher-income bedroom communities of Lafayette and Moraga, which adjoin Walnut Creek. These policies will limit the amount of diverse housing options that developers in these communities will be able to provide workers employed in Walnut Creek or Concord. To the extent they are provided, higher-density and other diverse housing options will continue to be concentrated in eastern Contra Costa communities like Antioch, which is now more than a half-hour's drive from downtown Walnut Creek. The unincorporated area east of San Ramon, which is located along I-680 and is within downtown Walnut Creek's 1990 half-hour driving time radius, anticipates significant future residential growth. As development takes place in unincorporated San Ramon, however, pressures on the freeway system will undoubtedly increase the driving time, making a commute to downtown Walnut Creek more onerous.

Policies and Housing in the Downtown Core

Walnut Creek's 1989 General Plan shifted the planning orientation of the downtown core from office to retail uses. To encourage more intense retail uses in the core area, the floor/area ratio in some retail areas (for example, the Golden Triangle area near the BART station) was increased in the 1989 General Plan. While retail FARs were in some instances increased, actual projects still had to meet the constraints on traffic and intersections posed by Measure H and in effect at that time. Before the 1989 General Plan, the FAR in the downtown was not a limiting factor, as most commercial space was not limited by the 2.5 FAR but by parking requirements. As commercial property increased in value, however, developers were willing to put in underground parking to build midrise structures. The community perceived these taller buildings as changing the character of downtown. The 1989 General Plan, therefore, actually decreased the FAR in most pedestrian retail areas.

The downtown core is bounded by Walden Avenue in the north, the Southern Pacific right-of-way to the east, and I-680 to the west. I-680 and the Southern Pacific right-of-way meet at the tip of the southern border. The dominant retail center is located along both sides of Main Street, between California and Broadway. The office-oriented Golden Triangle is bounded by I-680, Parkside, Main, California, and Pringle.

The Golden Triangle is where older housing stock, both single-family and lower-density multifamily units, were removed in the early 1980s to make way for higher-density office uses. The city encouraged mixed-use development at this site and required commercial developers either to provide replacement housing or to pay in-lieu fees, which was the route most office developers elected to take. To date, these housing fee monies have not been expended. One developer elected to create a building pad on top of his parking structure. The pad has been plumbed to receive approximately 40 dwellings, and entitlement is in place for the units that could be developed on the prepared pad. But according to the Planning Department, to date no one has been interested in building housing at that site. A mixed retail/multifamily development, Tower Court, however, has been developed in the area. The project has had financial difficulties, with present management taking over the development as part of a workout.

Tower Court opened in October 1991 and rented its 109 units within five months. Absorption was faster than had been anticipated, because one month after opening, the Oakland Hills fire forced households to seek immediate housing. The residential component of the development is still 100 percent leased, though the first-floor retail component is not. Negotiations have been completed for a restaurant to occupy part of the first floor.

Tower Court consists of 12 500-square-foot studio apartments renting for $590 to $715 per month, 70 one-bedroom units ranging from 650 to 730 square feet and leasing for $750 to $900 per month, and 27 two-bedroom units ranging from 830 to 930 square feet and leasing for $1,000 to $1,100 per month. Rents average about $1.25 per square foot, ranging from $1.13 to $1.49.

The typical renter in Tower Court is a one- or two-person household in the mid-30s with annual household income of $40,000 to $60,000. Most want to locate in Tower Court because of the development's proximity to a BART station. According to the apartment manager, this proximity to BART is far more important than the ready accessibility to downtown shopping and entertainment facilities—though proximity to three nearby health clubs is a marketing plus. Approximately one-half of the residents commute by BART to locations outside the market area, such as downtown San Francisco, about 20 percent commute to jobs located in the city of Walnut Creek, and the remainder travel to jobs within the commute shed. The manager believes that the closest competition for Tower Court is not other core area multi-family housing projects, but projects located near a BART station. Therefore, she believes the two closest competitors are Bay Landing and Treat Commons, two multi-family developments located near the Pleasant Hill BART station.

Other managers of multifamily developments in the core area reported similar demands. The typical renter in those developments is a one- or two-person household in the mid-30s with a relatively high income. They generally concur that, while being close to a BART station is an important factor, the majority of their renters do not work in Walnut Creek but commute to other locations. And nothing indicates that these households chose this lifestyle to reduce the necessity for an automobile. The other managers, however, did note that their renters found it more important to live in downtown activity centers. Living close to shopping and entertainment was a definite plus in their renters' decisions to locate in the downtown core.

Rental rates of some older multifamily units in the core were between $1.05 to $1.20 per square foot, somewhat below those charged at Tower Court. Some of the projects built recently have been mapped as condominiums so as to make conversion possible. But they currently are being rented, at relatively high occupancies.

Since 1990, only two near-downtown residential projects have been approved. The Oaks, a 36-affordable-unit development located on North Main Street, has received all of its planning approvals but is now waiting to see whether it can obtain the necessary low-income housing tax credits to make it work financially. The other downtown project approved since 1990 was a 174-unit project on Alma. It has not proceeded, and the city is unsure where the developer can be located.

Given the economics of development that have applied to Walnut Creek in recent years, however, it is not surprising that the project has not been built. Several existing projects, including Tower Court, have run into significant financial problems. In the case of Tower Court and several other downtown apartment/condominium projects, the original developer lost his equity and the property. The current operator of Tower Court provided the following estimates of the original developer's per-unit cost:

1. Land: $2.3 million ÷ 109 units = $21,100 per unit
2. Development cost, including fees and construction costs: $87,155 per unit
3. Fees and exactions and cost estimated for a 15-month period during which the developer sought to obtain approval for the project: $3,853 per unit
4. Total: $112,108 per unit

The operator of the project indicates that approval for the project could not have been received without the construction of street-level commercial space as required by the city, but the provision of ground-floor commercial space has tended to increase overall construction costs and required the developer to pay out $40 per square foot in tenant allowances. Furthermore, while the original pro forma indicated that rents on the main floor would be $2.25 per square foot, actual rents turned out to be $1.40 per square foot. Costs were also high because parking was constructed on top of the first-floor retail space, between the stores and residential units. Forty parking spaces were required to serve the commercial units. While the project's initiator had hoped to rent excess parking spaces to generate income during the day of about $50,000 per year, the actual revenue from parking has been about only $10,000 per year.

Even without the financially onerous requirement of ground-floor commercial space, it is very doubtful that land values and construction costs have decreased enough to make residential development feasible in an area that contains almost no vacant land and where older single-floor uses, such as single-family housing and motels, would have to be purchased and torn down to provide the land for new projects. Furthermore, the revisions to the city's General Plan have done nothing to decrease the costs imposed by municipal requirements in the core area. For example, Measure A lowered height limits in the Golden Triangle from 80 feet to 50 feet.

Nevertheless, the city has attempted to provide some incentive to construction by allowing density bonuses of up to 25 percent for residential development within 1,500 feet of the BART station. In most instances, it would also be possible for such development to meet the traffic standards that serve as an impediment to much high-density housing. In addition, the city would exempt projects that provide affordable housing from traffic intersection standards.

While it is difficult to predict that the future will not see some further high-density residential development in downtown Walnut Creek and elsewhere, given the strong demand for such housing, it is not likely that sufficient housing can be built to come even close to filling the gap between the supply of such units and the demand by commuters. The next section describes the effect that the existing gap between local jobs and housing affordable for those who hold the jobs has had on commutation patterns and vehicle-miles traveled.

The Effect of the Mismatch Between the Growth of Commercial and Residential Development

The lack of symmetry between the expansion of economic activities and the residential base of Walnut Creek and the communities around it has created patterns of commuting that adversely affect the region's traffic flows. One result of the increased number of workers and shoppers on the roads is suggested by the shrinkage of the distance that could be covered in 30 minutes of driving time between 1980 and 1990 (see Figure 2-12).

The dotted lines on the map indicate that, in 1980, one could drive to Walnut Creek within 30 minutes from the communities of Antioch, Pinole, Crockett, and Benicia,

all of which provided housing with prices below those that could be rented or purchased in Walnut Creek and the communities that adjoin it. By 1990, however, the increased traffic on the freeways had taken these communities out of the 30-minute driving time.

Figure 2-13 presents data obtained from the Metropolitan Transportation Commission (MTC), the Association of Bay Area Governments (ABAG), and the California Department of Finance to estimate the number of workers who commuted to and from Walnut Creek in 1980 and 1990. The number of persons living *and* working in Walnut Creek increased only 11.4 percent, or 909, between 1980 and 1990. This growth was slightly less than the increase in persons living in Walnut Creek but employed elsewhere. Out-commuters, who had always made up a larger portion of the local population than those who worked locally, increased by 5 percent in the decade. The percentage and number of persons employed in Walnut Creek but living elsewhere grew much more dramatically, however, climbing by close to 11,000 workers or over 40 percent in the decade.

Figure 2-14 shows the distance in miles traveled to work for all workers who live in Walnut Creek for 1980 and 1990. Distance is measured from Walnut Creek's civic center to the civic center where individuals work. In 1980, an employed resident of Walnut Creek traveled an average of 9.94 miles to work. The number of local residents who work within Walnut Creek or under five miles from it increased slightly, by 1.72 percent, and, most important, the average mileage traveled decreased by about 6 percent, to 9.36 miles.

Figure 2-15 presents estimates of the number of employees who work in Walnut Creek and how far they travel from work to home. For example, the first row of the figure presents an estimate of the number of people employed in Walnut Creek who live in the city itself or within surrounding areas under five miles from Walnut Creek's civic center. It is slightly larger than the number of individuals estimated on the first line of Figure 2-14, which refers to individuals who live in Walnut Creek itself and work in Walnut Creek or communities within five miles of the civic center. In contrast to employed residents of Walnut Creek, those who work in Walnut Creek and live elsewhere actually expanded the distance they commuted between 1980 and 1990 by 28.1 percent.

Figures 2-16 and 2-17 express the same pattern of commuting in terms of mean driving time in minutes rather than in miles. Again, as shown in Figure 2-16, the mean driving time for employed residents of Walnut Creek actually decreased slightly during the decade. If one could afford to live in Walnut Creek, the time spent

Figure 2-12

Approximate 30-Minute Driving Time Radius (1980 and 1990)

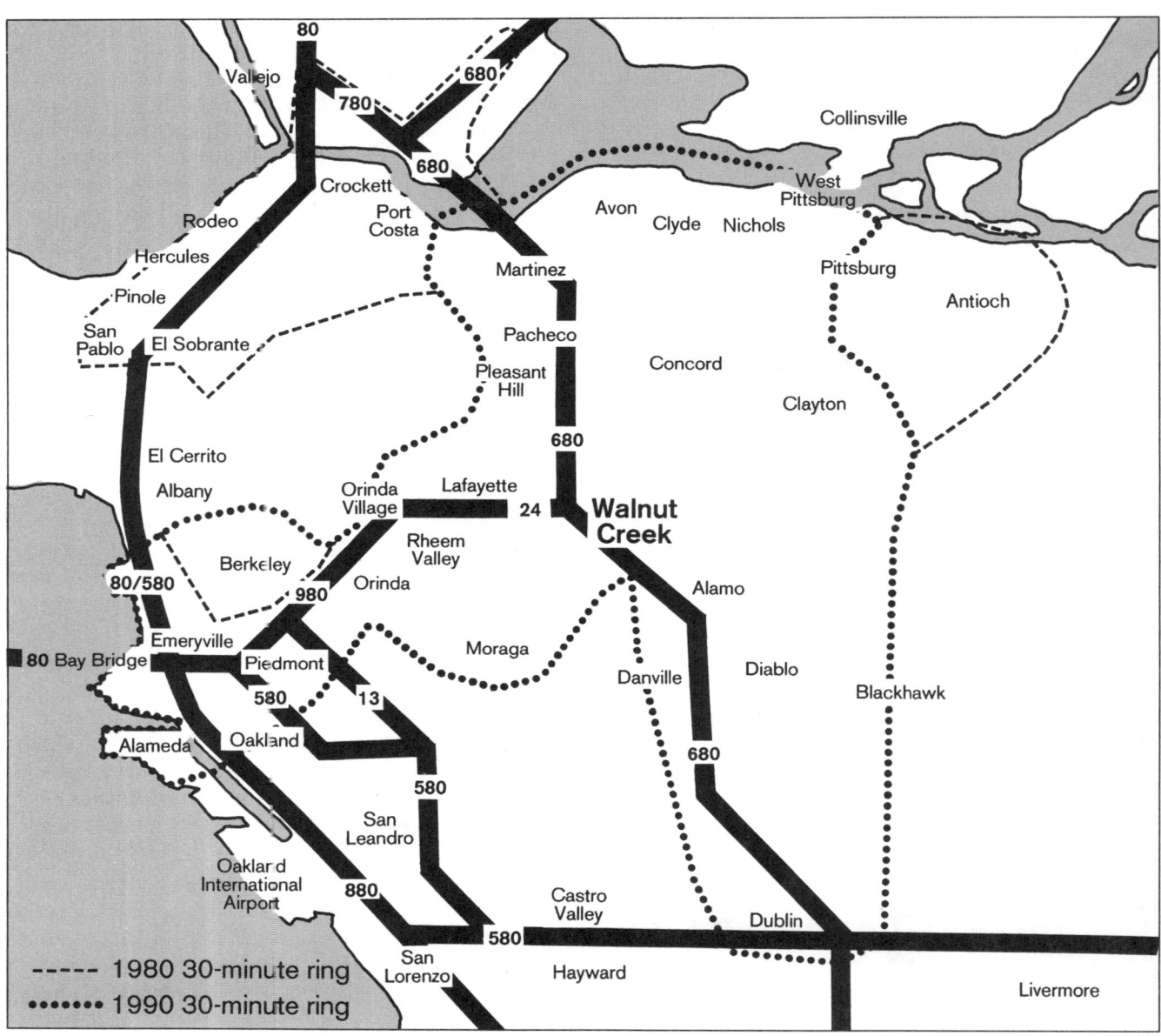

getting to work actually shrank a few seconds during the decade. Figure 2-17 shows the travel time of individuals working in Walnut Creek but living in the city and elsewhere. The travel time of this group increased by 20 percent during the decade. While at the beginning of the decade workers in Walnut Creek actually traveled less time from their residence than the average time spent getting to work by those who lived in Walnut Creek, at the end of the decade, the average travel times were very close.

Figures 2-18 and 2-19 present estimates of the average rents and home values of individuals employed in Walnut Creek categorized in terms of the relationship between these rents and values and the relative rents and values of houses in Walnut Creek. Median gross rents and prices were considered to be equivalent

Figure 2-13

Estimated Number of Workers Commuting to and from Walnut Creek (1980 and 1990)

	1980	1990	Change, 1980 to 1990	Percent Change, 1980 to 1990
Population of Walnut Creek	54,100	60,423	6,323	11.69
Persons Employed in Walnut Creek	35,201[1]	47,065[1]	11,864	33.70
Persons Employed in Walnut Creek but Living Elsewhere	27,242	38,197	10,955	40.21
Persons Living in Walnut Creek but Employed Elsewhere	20,293	21,308	1,015	5.00
Persons Living in Walnut Creek and Employed in Walnut Creek	7,959	8,868	909	11.42
Net Labor Force Imports[2]	6,949	16,889	9,940	143.04

[1]Excludes 900 persons employed in Walnut Creek but living outside the nine-county Bay Area. According to MTC, these data could undercount employment by 4 to 6 percent, because they are derived from U.S. Census data.
[2]"Net Labor Force Imports" is the number of "Persons Employed in Walnut Creek but Living Elsewhere" minus "Persons Living in Walnut Creek but Employed Elsewhere."
Sources: Metropolitan Transportation Commission; Gruen Gruen + Associates.

Figure 2-14

Distance between Place of Residence and Place of Work for All Workers Who Live in Walnut Creek (1980 and 1990)*

Distance Traveled to Work (Miles)	1980 Number of Commuters	1980 Percent of All Commuters	1990 Number of Commuters	1990 Percent of All Commuters	1980–1990 Percentage Change of All Commuters
Work in Walnut Creek or under 5	9,886	35.73	10,916	37.44	1.72
5 to 7.4	3,565	12.88	4,199	14.40	1.52
7.5 to 9.9	655	2.37	1,867	6.40	4.04
10 to 14.9	5,985	21.63	4,651	15.95	−5.68
15 to 19.9	756	2.73	1,163	3.99	1.26
20 to 29.9	6,496	23.48	5,761	19.76	−3.72
30 to 39.9	233	0.84	426	1.46	0.62
40 to 49.9	95	0.34	147	0.50	0.16
50 or More	0	0.00	24	0.08	0.08
Total	27,671	100.00	29,154	100.00	
Weighted Average (Miles)	9.94		9.36		−5.85

*Excludes Walnut Creek residents who work outside the nine-county Bay Area.
Note: Distance is measured from Civic Center to Civic Center for cities and Census-designated places.
Sources: Metropolitan Transportation Commission; California Dept. of Finance; Thomas Brothers Maps; Gruen Gruen + Associates.

Figure 2-15

Distance between Place of Residence and Place of Work for All Commuters Who Work in Walnut Creek (1980 and 1990)*

Distance Traveled to Home (Miles)	1980 Number of Commuters	1980 Percent of All Commuters	1990 Number of Commuters	1990 Percent of All Commuters	1980–1990 Percentage Change of All Commuters
Live in Walnut Creek or under 5	10,889	34.50	13,631	30.96	−3.54
5 to 7.4	9,897	31.36	11,694	26.56	−4.79
7.5 to 9.9	2,554	8.09	3,679	8.36	0.26
10 to 14.9	4,148	13.14	6,313	14.34	1.20
15 to 19.9	1,978	6.27	3,381	7.68	1.41
20 to 29.9	1,400	4.44	3,554	8.07	3.64
30 to 39.9	575	1.82	1,548	3.52	1.69
40 to 49.9	108	0.34	183	0.42	0.07
50 or More	14	0.04	42	0.10	0.05
Total	31,563	100.00	44,025	100.00	
Average Distance (Miles)	6.69		8.57		28.10

*Excludes workers living outside the nine-county Bay Area, approximately 900 people in 1990. Data for 1980 are unavailable.
Note: Distance is measured from Civic Center to Civic Center for cities and Census-designated places.
Sources: Metropolitan Transportation Commission; California Dept. of Finance; Thomas Brothers Maps; Gruen Gruen + Associates.

Figure 2-16

Mean Travel Time between Place of Residence and Place of Work for Automobile Commuters Who Live in Walnut Creek (1980 and 1990)*

Mean Travel Time (Minutes)	1980 Number of Automobile Commuters	1980 Percent of All Auto Commuters	1990 Number of Automobile Commuters	1990 Percent of All Auto Commuters	1980–1990 Percentage Change of All Auto Commuters
Under 15	7,501	33.74	6,852	28.16	−5.57
15 to 19.9	4,028	18.12	5,087	20.91	2.79
20 to 29.9	1,992	8.96	4,051	16.65	7.69
30 to 44.9	5,485	24.67	4,996	20.53	−4.14
45 to 59.9	3,084	13.87	3,002	12.34	−1.53
60 or More	144	0.65	342	1.41	0.76
Total	22,234	100.00	24,330	100.00	
Weighted Average (Minutes)	25.01		24.91		−0.38

*Excludes Walnut Creek residents who work outside the nine-county Bay Area.
Note: "Mean Travel Time" is for those commuting by automobile only.
Sources: Metropolitan Transportation Commission; California Dept. of Finance; Thomas Brothers Maps; Gruen Gruen + Associates.

Figure 2-17

Mean Travel Time between Place of Residence and Place of Work for Automobile Commuters Who Work in Walnut Creek (1980 and 1990)*

Mean Travel Time (Minutes)	1980 Number of Automobile Commuters	1980 Percent of All Auto Commuters	1990 Number of Automobile Commuters	1990 Percent of All Auto Commuters	1980–1990 Percentage Change of All Auto Commuters
Under 15	7,612	23.66	9,114	21.08	−2.58
15 to 19.9	13,515	42.01	13,761	31.83	−10.18
20 to 29.9	7,350	22.85	8,605	19.90	−2.94
30 to 44.9	2,930	9.11	9,294	21.50	12.39
45 to 59.9	507	1.58	2,170	5.02	3.44
60 or More	257	0.80	288	0.67	−0.13
Total	32,171	100.00	43,232	100.00	
Weighted Average (Minutes)	20.26		24.32		20.03

*Excludes workers living outside the nine-county Bay Area, approximately 900 people in 1990. Data for 1980 are unavailable.
Note: "Mean Travel Time" is for those commuting by automobile only.
Sources: Metropolitan Transportation Commission; California Dept. of Finance; Thomas Brothers Maps; Gruen Gruen + Associates.

if they fell within ±5 percent of Walnut Creek's rents and values.

Both Figures 2-18 and 2-19 allocate the 35,201 people estimated to have been employed in Walnut Creek in 1980 and the 47,065 people estimated to have worked in Walnut Creek in 1990 on the basis of the median rents and median home values of the communities where they reside relative to those rents and values in Walnut Creek. As suggested by Figure 2-18, 54 percent of all those employed in Walnut Creek in 1980 lived in communities whose rental housing was priced, on average, below that of Walnut Creek. As suggested by Figure 2-19, 68 percent of those who worked in Walnut Creek in 1980 lived in communities with home values below the average house in Walnut Creek.

By 1990, it was still true that more than half of all those employed in Walnut Creek lived in communities where rents were below the average in Walnut Creek, while 62 percent of those employed in the city, which is the focus of this analysis, resided in communities where houses cost less. On a rather trivial level, this categorization of data merely confirms the previously indicated finding that commuters driving relatively long distances to workplaces in Walnut Creek frequently do so to obtain more housing per dollar. Figures 2-18 and 2-19 suggest that the number of workers residing in com-

munities with less expensive for-sale and rental residential units had declined somewhat, leading to the hypothesis that, as driving time to communities with less expensive housing increases, the percentage of people who dig deeper in their pockets to avoid the extended commute tends to increase as well.

In sum, the relationships between patterns of commutation and available housing suggest that the pattern of residential land values and commuter patterns around the new activity center of Walnut Creek is similar to the pattern that William Alonzo observed around much older central cities in 1964, in *Location and Land Use*. Alonzo observed that residential land values tended to decrease as distance from the old center city workplaces increase so that, to obtain more land and house for their dollars, commuters had to travel farther. This phenomenon was partially explained by the fact that the transportation links tended to have been built out from the center city and that the amount of available land covered by a radius increases as one goes farther from the center. These same causes, however, appear not to have been nearly as important in the evolution of a similar situation in Walnut Creek.

Instead, what has happened is that the community of Walnut Creek and the communities around it have tended to preserve the more rural, relatively low-density hous-

▼▼▼

Figure 2-18

People Employed in Walnut Creek Categorized by Median Rent in Place of Residence (1980 and 1990)*

Rent Range	1980 Total Workers	1980 Percent of Total		1990 Total Workers	1990 Percent of Total	
Below 30 Percent of Walnut Creek Median	2,661	7.6		572	1.2	
20.1 to 30 Percent below Walnut Creek Median	1,528	4.3		2,947	6.3	
15.1 to 20 Percent below Walnut Creek Median	3,744	10.6		1,803	3.8	
10.1 to 15 Percent below Walnut Creek Median	3,988	11.3		4,194	8.9	
5.1 to 10 Percent below Walnut Creek Median	7,241	20.6	54.4%	15,463	32.9	53.1%
5 Percent below to 5 Percent above Walnut Creek Median (including Walnut Creek)	11,384	32.3	32.3%	10,395	22.1	22.1%
5.1 to 10 Percent above Walnut Creek Median	79	0.2	13.2%	4,504	9.6	24.8%
10.1 to 15 Percent above Walnut Creek Median	38	0.1		567	1.2	
15.1 to 20 Percent above Walnut Creek Median	11	0.0		659	1.4	
20.1 to 30 Percent above Walnut Creek Median	741	2.1		1,905	4.0	
Above 30 Percent of Walnut Creek Median	3,786	10.8		4,056	8.6	
Total	35,201	100.0	100.0%	47,065	100.0	100.0%

*Excludes workers living outside the nine-county Bay Area, approximately 900 people in 1990. Data for 1980 are unavailable.
Source: Gruen Gruen + Associates.

▲▲▲

ing patterns, with large amounts of open space that existed before the metamorphosis of Walnut Creek into an activity center or edge city. Richard Babcock, a land use attorney, in his 1966 book, *The Zoning Game,* referred to zoning as the weapon applied by suburbs to protect them from the central city. Suburban communities were enforcing a relative homogeneity in the economic and social classes they would allow to be housed within their communities—clearly at least an implicit goal of planning in Walnut Creek and nearby central Contra Costa County.

Thus, as their economic base changed and broadened, the residential markets they could serve remained relatively static. Even though more residents of Walnut Creek and the communities neighboring it now work in Walnut Creek than was the case in 1970 or 1980, the range of affordable housing continues to fit best within the purchasing power of relatively affluent commuters living in a bedroom community. The role that BART has played has been to facilitate not only the commuting of workers and customers who live elsewhere, but also the commutes of those who want to live in a pleasant environment and can afford to do so.

Lost and Remaining Opportunities

Decisions and actions taken by local communities often result in unexpected impacts over time, and policies and regulations that might have a beneficial effect in the short term might become increasingly deleterious in the longer term. In the same vein, what might be positive policy from a local jurisdiction's perspective could have a negative impact on the region's economy. For example, providing high-density housing to serve moderate-income families might have a negative fiscal impact on the local community's fiscal health. But when multiple jurisdictions decide to curtail this type of housing, the economy of the region suffers from a shortage of close-in diverse wokers as well as from the negative impacts of longer and more onerous commutes.

If a full spectrum of housing choices is not provided as this country's suburban places change from primarily bedroom communities to regional activity centers, then commutation must necessarily result in a cross-quilt pattern. The historic pattern of residential commu-

Figure 2-19

People Employed in Walnut Creek Categorized by Median Home Value in Place of Residence (1980 and 1990)*

Home Value Range	1980 Total Workers	1980 Percent of Total		1990 Total Workers	1990 Percent of Total	
Below 30 Percent of Walnut Creek Median	15,628	44.4		20,880	44.4	
20.1 to 30 Percent below Walnut Creek Median	5,645	16.0		6,414	13.6	
15.1 to 20 Percent below Walnut Creek Median	1,714	4.9		336	0.7	
10.1 to 15 Percent below Walnut Creek Median	87	0.2		814	1.7	
5.1 to 10 Percent below Walnut Creek Median	848	2.4	68.0%	747	1.6	62.0%
5 Percent below to 5 Percent above Walnut Creek Median (including Walnut Creek)	7,156	20.3	20.3%	11,175	23.7	23.7%
5.1 to 10 Percent above Walnut Creek Median	26	0.1	11.7%	950	2.0	14.2%
10.1 to 15 Percent above Walnut Creek Median	51	0.1		184	0.4	
15.1 to 20 Percent above Walnut Creek Median	2,435	6.9		120	0.3	
20.1 to 30 Percent above Walnut Creek Median	1,056	3.0		1,367	2.9	
Above 30 Percent of Walnut Creek Median	555	1.6		4,078	8.7	
Total	35,201	100.0	100.0%	47,065	100.0	100.0%

*Excludes workers living outside the nine-county Bay Area, approximately 900 people in 1990. Data for 1980 are unavailable.
Source: Gruen Gruen + Associates.

nities radiating outward from larger-scale central cities will continue to weaken over time. The extent to which regional activity centers will be able to replace the multiple commercial and institutional functions these center cities once provided will depend on the diversity of economic opportunities, including a broad range of housing, that is provided within and around these activity centers.

If Walnut Creek and the communities around it had maintained their vision of the holding capacity of their communities that had been evidenced in the planning that was done in the 1960s and 1970s, a greater amount and range of housing could have been supplied than what has been produced. If the old vision of residential carrying capacity had stayed in place, or even been increased, real estate developers would have been in a stronger position to expand the production of higher-density housing. These potential supplies would have become reality because of the increase in demand for housing at a wide variety of price ranges that was induced by the increase in jobs generated by the metamorphosis of Walnut Creek. But the vision of how many houses the land could accommodate was consistently shrunk over the years, both within

Walnut Creek and the other relatively high-income communities bordering it. As a result, the opportunity for developing a large group of heterogeneous neighborhoods serving the same range of incomes provided by increasing job opportunities in Walnut Creek never became a reality.

Furthermore, this opportunity seems to have been lost for the foreseeable future. No evidence exists of any efforts to alter the economics of development that have been put in place by a combination of public policy and the pattern of residential development. For example, relatively little vacant land is zoned for higher-density residential development in the downtown, and some of that land has other, nonresidential uses. The political and dollar costs of demolishing existing older, relatively obsolete, and lower-density residential and commercial uses and replacing them with higher-density multifamily structures are also relatively great. The general requirement for first-floor commercial space raises the risks and costs of such projects. Thus, both economically and politically, the guidelines being laid down for development are for the slow growth of residences similar to the products and price ranges of today.

Without public subsidy to write down the cost of land, the realities of the market will preclude the development of new high-density multifamily housing in downtown Walnut Creek until rents rise over present levels. Therefore, it seems unlikely that the present range of affordability will be widened. By not providing significantly increased opportunities for households to live downtown, Walnut Creek officials minimize the magnitude of its future daytime and nighttime population base, as well as the opportunity to help ease future traffic congestion.

Existing residents, however, have adopted another means to lower congestion by limiting both commercial and residential development within their community, including the downtown. City officials understand that, if they lessen future development and employment, less stress will be placed on their roadway and transit systems. A policy to limit the magnitude of both future commercial development and high-density housing will not have a deleterious impact on Walnut Creek's economic well-being in the short run and might have only minimum negative impacts in the long run. Such a policy to limit growth, however, will tend to alter future land use and transportation patterns within the region as future employment growth takes place in a variety of smaller-scale activity centers, none of them able to approach the scale and diversity of the historic center city.

This emerging land use pattern of scattered suburban activity centers is likely to induce an increasing pattern of congestion as fewer and fewer households will have the opportunity of working within a close commute of home. Once such patterns are formed, the problems of congestion are unlikely to be solved without very heavy expenditures for added roadways and transit systems. Further, as the commutation from areas that provide less expensive houses continues to take more time, the availability of labor will decrease, while the cost of labor will tend to rise, making the region's economy less competitive in the global market. Some pundits say this situation is already contributing to the present downturn of California's economy.

The strength shown by the evolution of cities like Walnut Creek into activity centers and the comparative advantages they enjoy over the center city strongly suggest that this pattern cannot be avoided merely by strengthening the center city. Instead, if a more efficient and comfortable long-run pattern of living and working is to evolve, the land use policies of suburban activity centers with regard to housing have to change dramatically. Rather than provide token support for small amounts of affordable housing induced through inclusionary zoning or subsidization, planning for and allowing the expansion of both the number and diversity of neighborhoods built around these suburban activity centers must escalate dramatically. If communities like Walnut Creek elect to curtail the growth of their activity centers, the future pattern of land use in suburbia will be a multiplicity of smaller, less functionally diverse activity centers tied together by increasingly congested highways.

Notes

1. In 1985, the citizens of Walnut Creek passed growth-restricting Measure H, which was enforced until it was overturned by the California Supreme Court in December 1990. Measure H limited commercial and residential development based on traffic congestion. No buildings or structures were to be built if the peak-hour vehicle-to-capacity ratio of all intersections on Ygnacio Valley Road and within the core area was 0.85 or less. Measure H prohibited estimates based on introducing transportation system management programs. Certain uses were exempted, such as housing for senior citizens and health and safety institutions.

2. A buildout of 56,750 units, or almost twice the number of units that exist today, was contemplated in 1971 for the planning area. The planning area is estimated to account for about 19 percent of this housing stock.

Chapter 3

▲▲▲▲▲▲▲▲▲▲

City Centre Southfield, Michigan

by
Richard C. Ward and Barry Hogue

**Development Strategies, Inc.
St. Louis, Missouri**

The case study of City Centre was completed in April 1994.

Introduction

This housing study of Southfield, Michigan, one of Detroit's inner ring of suburbs, is one of four such studies commissioned by ULI. The objectives of the Southfield case study were to examine how the combination of market factors, demographic forces, and public policy decisions influenced the development of higher-density housing in Southfield and then, by evaluating potential market demand, supply, and other impediments to and opportunities for development, to suggest strategies for accommodating and encouraging additional higher-density housing development in the area of Southfield City Centre. A further objective was to draw upon the understanding gained from this case study to suggest how the opportunities and strategies identified in Southfield can be employed to encourage increased higher-density housing development in other suburban employment centers.

Rationale for Selecting Southfield as a Case Study

The city of Southfield has a population just over 75,000 in a metropolitan area of 4.36 million. The community's most distinctive characteristic, however, is the presence of over 24 million square feet of office space. Southfield

▼▼▼▼▼▼▼▼▼▼▼▼▼▼▼▼▼▼▼▼▼▼▼▼▼▼▼▼▼▼▼

**Figure 3-1
The Study Area**

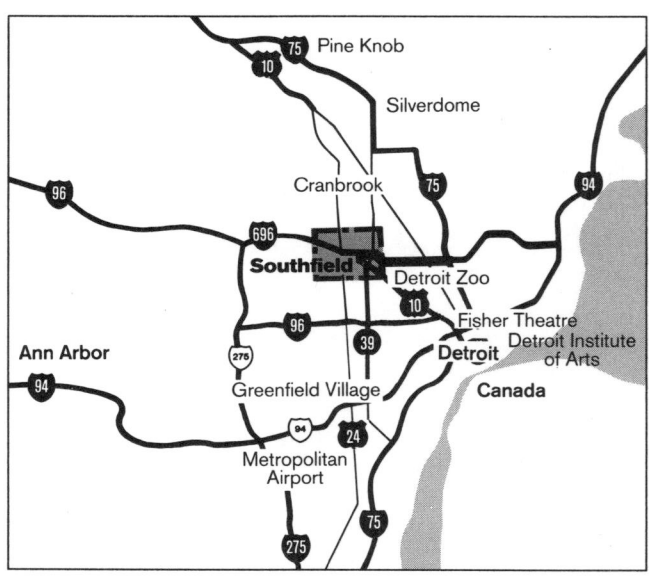

▲▲▲▲▲▲▲▲▲▲▲▲▲▲▲▲▲▲▲▲▲▲▲▲▲▲▲▲▲▲▲

Figure 3-2
Higher-Density Units

Jurisdiction	Total Housing Units	Single Family (Percent)	Condominium (Percent)	Multifamily Rental (Percent)
Oakland County	432,700	76	3	21
Southfield	35,100	52	6	42
Farmington Hills	31,200	60	5	35
Novi	13,600	71	4	25
Royal Oak	29,200	66	6	28
Troy	27,200	80	2	18
West Bloomfield	20,400	69	23	8

has evolved since the late 1950s as the most significant suburban employment center in the Detroit metropolitan area. In the early 1960s, the community's elected officials made a conscious policy decision to plan for and accommodate the pattern of office development that was emerging along Northwestern Highway (M-10), opened in 1960 as an extension to the John Lodge Expressway. Also as part of the plan, Southfield's officials decided to seek to accommodate higher-density multifamily housing associated with the growth of office employment in the community.

The result of that decision is that Southfield today offers the broadest selection of higher-density housing products available in any community in the suburban Detroit market. The city's combined rental and ownership multifamily units represent approximately one-half of its total housing stock, highest of any community in Oakland County, where three-fourths of the housing is comprised of detached single-family houses.

Today, some of Southfield's multifamily units are approaching 30 years in age and need major reinvestment. Likewise, demographic changes are producing more tenants, with families occupying units originally designed for wealthy couples and single tenants without children. These issues and others related to public schools, increasing racial diversity, and the decreasing availability of land for additional higher-density housing have caused Southfield's city officials to reevaluate the city's policies regarding accommodating or encouraging new higher-density residential development.

Another factor contributing to the importance of reevaluating the market and public policy issues related to higher-density housing in Southfield is the recent completion of a plan for the city's office core, called City Centre. The City Centre Plan recommends adding vitality to the office core area by introducing more retailing, restaurants, entertainment, and housing to the area. The residential densities required to support such uses and land costs in City Centre will mean additional higher-density housing. The target markets, potential demand, housing products, design, and location become important considerations, even as the city reassesses its policy toward allowing more multifamily development.

Approach and Methodology

The approach to the case study was to examine the market, public policy, and other forces behind historic development patterns in Southfield. Next, the housing component proposed in the City Centre Plan was used as a framework for evaluating the market potential, issues, and impediments to developing new higher-density residential housing in and around the office employment core. Preparing the case study included collecting historic development data, reviewing market information and city plans and policies, interviewing over 20 real estate professionals and city officials, including the mayor, the City

Figure 3-3
Southfield City Centre Core Area

Centre advisory board, and planning and community development directors, and conducting an attitudinal survey of 1,100 employees who work in the City Centre area.

Key Issues

Several key issues were addressed in the Southfield case study:

▼ What is the potential demand for higher-density housing in City Centre?

▼ How does Southfield's past policy of accommodating multifamily development and the city's existing relatively high percentage of such housing affect the present and future potential for development?

▼ How does the supply of existing units and the city's historic pattern of development influence City Centre's competitive position and potential for development?

▼ What are the primary impediments to capitalizing on the potential demand for additional higher-density housing in City Centre?

▼ What public policy initiatives and private development strategies can most effectively mitigate the development impediments and realize the benefits of higher-density housing in Southfield's City Centre?

▼ Which of the initiatives and strategies aimed at increasing higher-density residential development in City Centre are likely to be applicable to other suburban activity centers?

Southfield's Evolution As a Suburban Employment Center in the Detroit Metropolitan Area

Historic Development

The city of Southfield is adjacent to Detroit's northwestern corporate boundary in Oakland County, one of the four counties making up the Detroit MSA. The MSA has a population of approximately 4.36 million people, an increase over 1970 (3.99 million) and slightly fewer than 1980 (4.48 million). The region ranks among the nation's top six or seven metropolitan areas based on demographic measures of population, households, income, and retail sales. Detroit's economy has traditionally been built on the automobile industry, and though economic diversification is apparent, automobile production remains the region's primary industry.

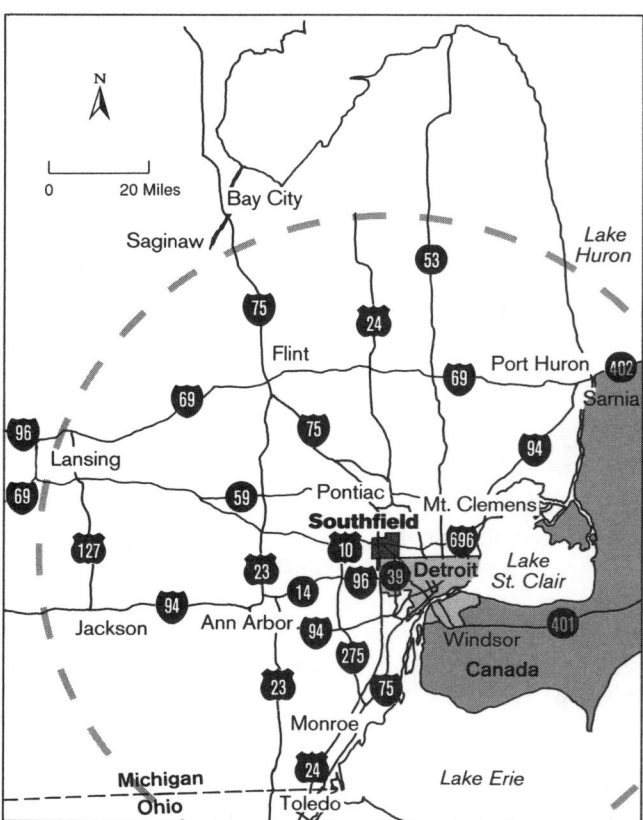

Figure 3-4
Seventy-Mile Radius of Southfield

Southfield was one of the first communities to benefit from the rapid suburbanization of the Detroit region that began in the mid-1950s and accelerated in the 1960s. Northland Center, the nation's first regional shopping center, opened in 1954 and became a catalyst for a development boom that rapidly swept the newly incorporated (1958) city of Southfield. Initially, retail and office development was concentrated in the 400-acre area surrounding Northland Center, near the intersection of Southfield Road (M-39) and Eight Mile Road (M-102), Detroit's northern boundary.

Office Development

With the opening in 1960 of Northwestern Highway, major corporate office centers began to locate along what has been termed the "Golden Corridor." Standard Oil, Bendix Corporation, Allstate Insurance, Maccabees Mutual Life Insurance Company, and Federal Mogul

Figure 3-5
Office Development in Southfield

Year	Office Space Constructed Annually (Square Feet)	Total Office Space Available (Square Feet)
1960	346,380	979,351
1965	506,457	2,313,683
1970	1,199,678	7,939,991
1975	1,580,381	12,004,389
1980	328,206	14,156,622
1985	1,810,409	19,476,850
1990	416,036	23,569,974

Corporation are but a few of the many prominent firms that selected office sites adjacent to Northwestern Highway. Growth was dramatic, with total office space exploding from 600,000 square feet in 1959 to 7.9 million square feet by 1970.

Office development continued at a similar pace through the 1970s, when another 6.2 million square feet was added to the inventory, bringing the total to 14.1 million square feet by 1980. It was apparent by this time that the land use pattern created by office development was focused on the half-square-mile triangle formed by Northwestern Highway, Eleven Mile Road, and Evergreen Road. A number of Southfield's most significant corporate and speculative office buildings would ultimately be located within or adjacent to that area, which would become known as Southfield City Centre. Throughout the 1980s, when another 9.9 million square feet of office space was developed in the city, the City Centre area continued to attract office development. Today, approximately 5 million square feet of Southfield's 24 million square feet of office space

(nearly 21 percent) is contained within the one square mile around City Centre. Four of the city's eight office buildings over 500,000 square feet are located in the City Centre area, including Prudential Town Center, Allied Automotive Center, Northwestern Office Centre, and the Travelers/EDS towers. Southfield's 24 million square feet of office space is approximately 40 percent of the total office inventory in the four-county Detroit MSA. Of this 24 million square feet, approximately 4 million square feet is owner-occupied, with the remaining 20 million square feet available for general occupancy.

Residential Development around Employment Centers

Housing development, especially the construction of multifamily rental units, has been driven by office development. In 1960, Southfield contained 8,500 single-family detached houses and only 30 multifamily units. During the 1960s, over 5,000 multifamily units were constructed in Southfield, including the Detroit market's first luxury high-rise apartments, North Park Towers. These 14- and 20-story towers with 750 units, located adjacent to Northland Center, attracted wealthy tenants, typically mature couples without children. Development of single-family detached houses also increased rapidly in the 1960s, almost doubling from 8,500 in 1960 to 16,700 in 1970. Multifamily development took another quantum leap in the 1970s, reaching 14,800 units by 1980, while single-family detached development rose by only about 1,300 units during that ten-year period. During the 1980s, as approximately 10 million square feet of office space was constructed in Southfield, some 2,000 additional multifamily units and about 150 single-family detached units were built.

Throughout the three decades from 1960 to 1990, multifamily housing continually increased as a percentage of Southfield's housing stock. In 1960, multifamily units

Figure 3-6
Population and Housing in Southfield (1960 to 1990)

	Population	Households	Persons per Household	Single-Family Units	Multifamily Units	Office Space (Square Feet)
1960	31,500	8,770	3.59	8,466	30	980,000
1970	69,000	20,380	3.39	16,730	5,171	7,900,000
1980	75,600	30,240	2.50	18,046	14,797	14,100,000
1990	75,700	32,360	2.34	18,200	16,859	24,000,000

Figure 3-7

Higher-Density Residential Development near Employment Centers

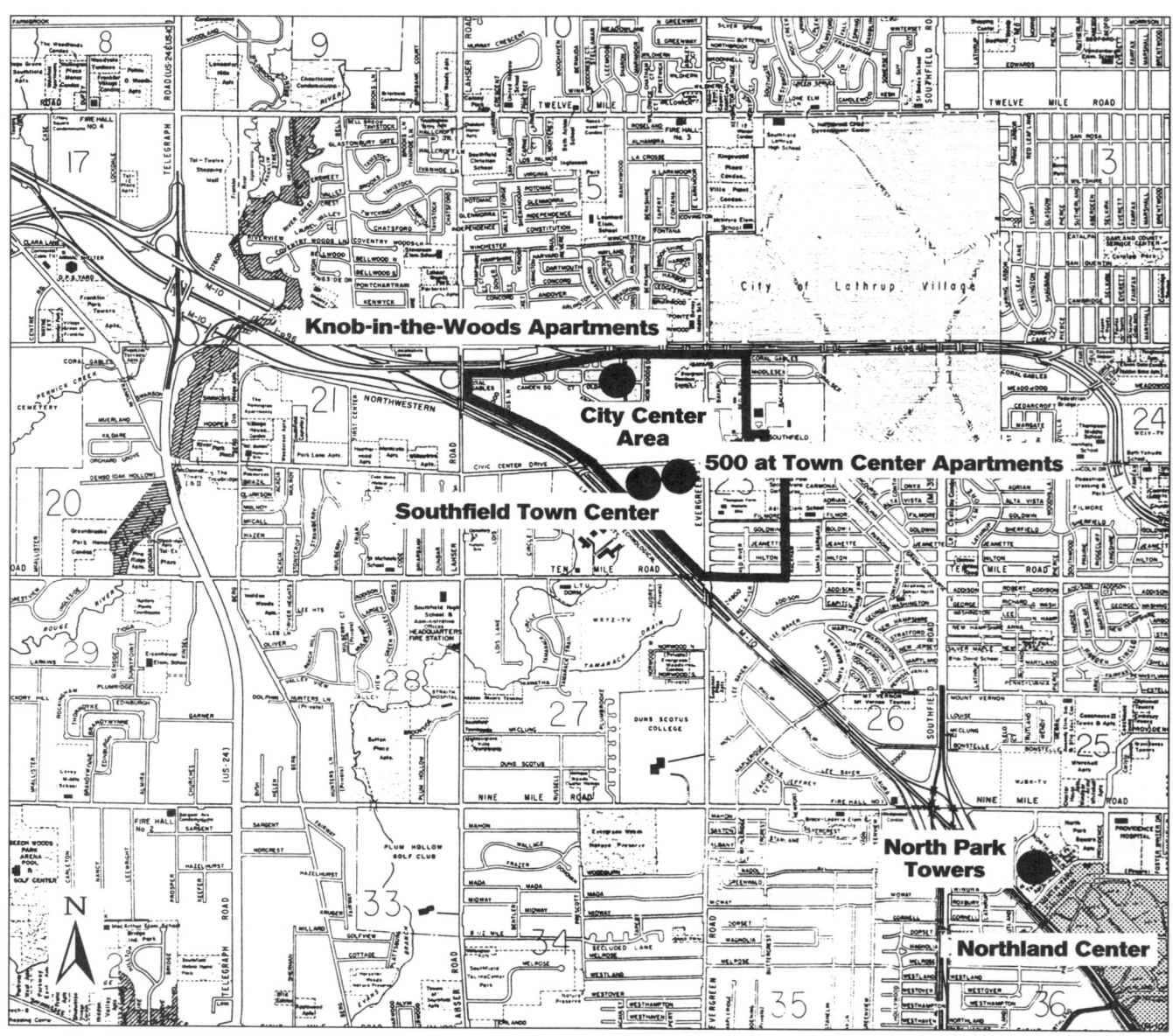

represented less than 1 percent of Southfield's housing, but by 1970 it had grown to 24 percent and by 1980 to 45 percent, leveling off at approximately 48 percent by 1990. Southfield has historically led Detroit suburban communities in higher-density housing, both in terms of annual production and as a percentage of overall housing stock. Though several other communities in Oakland County (Troy, Farmington Hills, and Auburn Hills, for example) have produced more multifamily units in the last few years, Southfield still leads suburban communities in total higher-density units and in the percentage of housing that is multifamily units (48 percent of all Southfield's housing compared to 40 percent in Farmington Hills, which ranks second).

Southfield's higher-density housing covers a broad range of housing types and prices: garden apartments, three-story elevator units, high-rise apartment towers, and residential developments for senior citizens in a variety of configurations. The city's multifamily housing is comprised largely of rental apartments; only about 12 percent are ownership units, reflecting that type's limited acceptance in the region and in the Midwest. Despite the high number and percentage of higher-density units, they are generally widely dispersed throughout the city's 27 square miles. Only North Park Towers and North Park Square Apartments near Northland Center and perhaps 5000 at Town Center Apartments and Knob-in-the-Woods Apartments near City Centre would be considered clustered near office employment centers.

Public Policy Regarding Multifamily Development

Southfield's evolution as a suburban employment center, including its accommodation of higher-density housing, is especially noteworthy, as the city's planning staff and elected officials anticipated and planned for it. Planning for the community as it is today began in the 1950s and 1960s, when Northland Center and adjacent properties were being developed. Well-conceived land use plans and development regulations formed a solid basis for the city's physical growth. Planners anticipated opportunities for development created by major roadway improvements and extensions, and this legacy of responsible planning and vision for the future has continued in Southfield to the present. The Downtown Development Authority's accomplishments, the newly adopted City Centre Plan, and the cooperative multijurisdiction redevelopment along Eight Mile Road are testimony to the city's efforts and success in effectively planning and guiding its growth and development.

One important aspect of Southfield's early planning was the decision to incorporate and accommodate multifamily housing in the community's future development. According to Donald Fracassi, mayor of Southfield since 1975, some of the city's earliest political battles centered around the issue of whether, and to what extent, the community should accommodate multifamily housing. The standard arguments about apartment tenants' being more transient and not having a stake in the community were voiced. Ultimately, however, the benefits to the city seemed compelling to residents and their leaders: apartments (there were no condominiums or cooperatives at the time) were incubators for single-family homeownership; apartments were fiscal winners in that they would

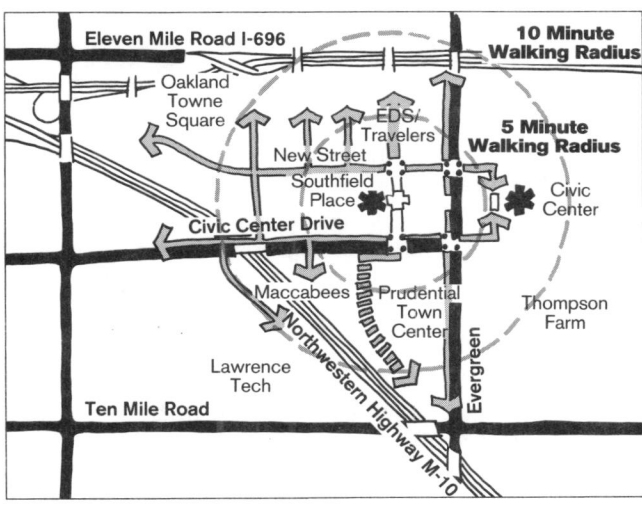

Figure 3-8
City Centre Core Area

generate more revenue than they required in services, because few tenants had school-age children and many amenities, such as tennis courts and swimming pools, were provided by the developer; multifamily housing was in demand as a result of the concentration of office and retail workers; and financial institutions were willing to lend money for apartment projects. The proponents of multifamily development prevailed, and Southfield incorporated higher-density residential development into its land use planning, zoning, and other policy and regulatory framework. Almost from the city's incorporation, higher-density housing did not just happen but was a response to market demand and a conscious decision by the city to accommodate it.

The most recent public policy debate regarding higher-density housing arose in 1989 as part of the planning for City Centre. Within the core area of the 850 acres are to be a concentration of public spaces, civic buildings, and high-density housing, along with retail space, parking, restaurants, and entertainment. They are to be assembled on a gridded street system that provides a pedestrian-oriented environment. This plan is designed to be superimposed on the present pattern of development in the City Centre area, which consists primarily of freestanding office towers, parking lots, and limited restaurant and retail development. The two major residential developments in the core area are the 34-story 5000 at Town Center residential apartment tower (originally marketed as condominiums) and Knob-in-the-Woods, a high-quality garden apartment development on the north edge of the City Centre core area. Additional high-density residential development has been proposed for the core area to help create the concentration of people that will lend vitality and patronage to the mixed-use environment. The plan suggests that roughly 900 additional new units be added to the City Centre core. Approximately 200 of them could be provided in a companion residential tower adjacent to the 5000 at Town Center building, with the balance in three- to five-story structures on Evergreen Avenue and one building on the proposed new east/west street in the core area.

Another issue facing Southfield concerns the age, condition, and occupancy of some of the older multifamily housing stock, some of which is approaching 30 years in age. As mentioned, most of these older apartments were designed for and marketed to younger and older couples and singles without children. Several factors, however, have combined to change the tenant profile in many of the apartment developments. The regional economic impact of the auto industry's scaling back and deteriorating conditions in many of Detroit's inner-city neighborhoods have prompted many former Detroit residents, including African-American and other ethnic groups, to look to Southfield's excellent public schools and good housing stock as a viable option for living, working, and raising families. While Southfield's many apartments offer an economical way to establish residency and enroll children in the school system, many of the apartments now occupied by families with children were not designed with adequate space, recreation areas, and other features needed to accommodate children. The age of some of the buildings and their changing occupancy have created maintenance headaches and other problems the city is wrestling with. These problems and the 50/50 split between Southfield's single-family and multifamily housing have caused some residents and civic leaders to look more favorably on the development of more multifamily housing—certain to be a controversial issue when rezoning proposals to allow higher-density housing in City Centre are reviewed.

Current and Projected Demand for Higher-Density Housing in the City Centre Area

This section examines potential housing demand in the City Centre area from two perspectives. First, it evaluates the general multifamily market and factors affecting potential demand in Southfield. Second, it draws upon the results of a market survey of City Centre employees conducted as part of this case study.

Market Factors Influencing Demand

In the late 1980s, the market for multifamily rental and condominium units in Southfield began to soften, and the softening was apparent even before the worst of the national recession affected suburban Detroit housing markets. To some extent, it was attributable to overbuilding but equally important was the competition from new multifamily units in surrounding communities, particularly Farmington Hills, Novi, Troy, and Auburn Hills. While current economic conditions have slowed the production of higher-density housing and will help reduce the excess supply, competition from new projects in nearby communities will continue to be high, even as economic conditions affecting housing production improve.

Other critical factors influencing current and future demand in Southfield include the perception of the community as a whole and the quality and condition of existing higher-density housing in general. If the issues of older apartment units and the impacts of more families' occupying units ill-suited for children are left unaddressed, the real and perceived problems they create will hurt Southfield's image and could ultimately reduce demand for higher-density housing, including that proposed for City Centre.

As new roadways and improved highways once contributed to Southfield's accessibility and demand for development, newly constructed routes are also opening once distant undeveloped areas for increasing suburban expansion. Or, as one seasoned apartment developer stated, "The same roads that once brought new residents to Southfield have now been extended to carry them out of town if they so choose." The recent completion of I-696, for example, reduces commuting times (at least for now) for some seeking greener residential pastures.

During the last multifamily development cycle, suburban residential developers, including those building in Southfield, responded to market demand by producing internally oriented two- and three-story garden apartment developments at densities of 12 to 15 dwelling units per acre. Condominium projects developed during that cycle were typically small, fewer than 20 units in most cases, at approximately the same densities as the garden apartment projects. Multifamily development of this configuration and relatively low density, however, is inconsistent with the character and development economics envisioned for the City Centre core. In fact, the higher-density residences proposed for City Centre's core are not well represented in the suburban marketplace today. Units are anticipated to be a combination of high-rise units as well as four- to five-story units. In some cases, they might be located over retail uses to create the required density needed to enhance patronage for retail and service uses and to bring per-unit residential land costs to a feasible level. But effective demand for this type of higher-density residential product remains in question, because it has had very limited exposure to the marketplace in recent years.

The survey of employees described in the following section was designed to help evaluate the potential market for the higher-density residential products envisioned for City Centre.

A Survey of City Centre Employees

In August 1993, approximately 1,100 survey forms were distributed to City Centre employees to elicit their interest in, attitudes about, and preferences for higher-density housing with supporting retail and entertainment uses in the City Centre area. The Southfield Community Development Department worked cooperatively with City Centre employers. This section of the report describes the results of the survey and analyzes those results. In its assessment of the market potential for higher-density housing in City Centre, the survey provides a valuable indicator of the demand for the proposed product.

Response Rate
Of the 1,100 survey forms distributed to downtown employees, 190 were completed and returned, a 17 percent response rate. Responses reflected a range of employee types, from management and administrative personnel to professional and clerical employees. The low response rate could be because some employees already reside in the City Centre area or, perhaps, because overall interest is lower.

Interest in Living in City Centre
Of the 190 survey respondents, 59 people (31 percent) replied "yes" or "maybe" when asked whether they would consider renting or buying a newly constructed residence in the City Centre area (14 percent "yes," 17 percent "maybe"). The survey was designed to sample a group representative of City Centre's employee population; hence, it could be optimistically concluded that 31 out of 100 people working in the City Centre area make up a potential market of "interested" households.

A potential market pool of City Centre employees who would consider living downtown could be estimated at approximately 6,200 persons, based on the following assumptions:

▼ A City Centre workforce estimated at 20,000 employees;
▼ Thirty-one percent of the employees sampled who would consider living in City Centre;
▼ Thirty-one percent of 20,000 equals 6,200;
▼ The primary market for housing in City Centre would include those households in which at least one person works in the City Centre area.

This approach is, of course, optimistic when evaluating the potential market pool of employees. Another, more conservative, method would be to assume that all employees who did not complete and return the survey forms were "not interested" in City Centre housing. Thus, only 59 out of 1,100 were interested (5.4 percent). Applying this percentage to the 20,000-person City Centre workforce results in a potential housing market pool of approximately 1,080. Realistically, the size of the potential market probably lies somewhere between 6,200 and 1,080. This potential housing market pool of City Centre employees is further qualified by additional factors discussed in subsequent parts of this section. Also to be considered is the reality that others who do not now work in City Centre or Southfield would be attracted to new residential products in the City Centre area. With over 24 million square feet of office space in Southfield, this larger market itself represents approximately 96,000 employees.

Preferred Type of Unit
The survey asked employees what types of housing they would prefer and listed 11 different types, from townhouses for sale through high-rise apartments for rent. Respondents were allowed to indicate their preferences by ranking their choices as "first," "second," or "third" and were allowed to make multiple choices. The top "first choices" are shown in Figure 3-9.

When general housing types are combined, without regard for numbers of bedrooms or other factors, both mid-/high-rise apartments and townhouses outscore garden apartments by a wide margin. While this response could relate to the number of choices offered for each housing type in the summary, it is an interesting result in a residential market that has recently produced only garden apartments. It is also encouraging, as the preferred types are consistent with the higher-density residential uses envisioned for City Centre.

Another approach to evaluating the preferences for type of unit is to examine the total number of first, second, or third choices received by each housing type. Two-bedroom mid-/high-rise apartments still tie for first place

Figure 3-9
Employees' First Choices for Type of Housing

First Choice Ranking	Building Type	Bedrooms/ Bathrooms	Sale or Rent
1	Mid-/High-Rise	2/1.5	Rent
2	Townhouse	2/2	Rent
3	Townhouse	2/1.5	Rent
4	Townhouse	2/2	Sale
5	Townhouse	3/2.5	Sale
6	Garden Apartment	1/1	Rent
7	Townhouse	3/2	Rent
8	Garden Apartment	2/1	Rent
9	Mid-/High-Rise	2/2	Sale
10	Mid-/High-Rise	1/1	Rent
11	Mid-/High-Rise	2/1	Rent

using this approach, but townhouses and even two-bedroom garden apartments rate equally high.

The results of respondents' answers point to several key observations:

▼ Additional analysis of preferences for type of unit indicate that respondents are typically income-qualified; that is, the rents or mortgages for the preferred unit types represent no more than 25 percent of their incomes. Significantly, 61 percent of the "interested" respondents have annual household incomes of $40,000 or above.

▼ Among rental units, the top preferences are two-bedroom mid-/high-rise apartments and two-bedroom townhouses.

▼ Two- and three-bedroom townhouses are the preferred ownership types indicated in the survey.

▼ Among those who answered "yes" rather than "maybe" to the question about interest in a new residence in City Centre, mid-/high-rise apartments with 1.5 baths for rent rate highest of the housing types listed by a margin of over 2 to 1.

▼ The least-preferred rental housing types are mid-/high-rise apartments for rent with a single bathroom, garden apartments, and three-bedroom townhouses.

Desired Housing Features

The results of questions related to services and amenities available or planned for the City Centre area are shown in Figure 3-10. Among these features, access to recreation facilities and to cultural and entertainment facilities, including a public library, are the most important. Access to daycare and walking distance to work are the least important features to those interested in living downtown. Access to health care services receives generally favorable responses.

Twenty features of housing units were included in the survey to evaluate their relative importance to interested respondents. Figure 3-11 illustrates the top ten highest-rated features. Over 50 percent of the interested respondents rated living room size, number of bathrooms, washer/dryer furnished, walk-in closets, and nearby supermarkets "important" or "very important" features. Individual garages, nearby assigned parking spaces, electronic security systems, kitchen size and design, and balcony/deck all were "important" or "very important" to over 40 percent of those responding.

On the low end of the scale, valet parking, a tot lot or playground, and a computer/business room in the clubhouse were the three least important features.

Figure 3-10
Importance of Housing Features in City Centre

	Not Important					Very Important		
	0	1	2	3	4	5	Total Replies	Mean
Walking Distance to Work	25	8	9	13	4	7	66	1.76
Culture and Entertainment	6	3	8	21	12	15	65	3.15
Access to Daycare	39	3	3	7	6	5	63	1.25
Access to Health Care	14	5	6	15	10	13	63	2.65
Access to Library	6	5	8	16	21	10	66	3.08
Access to Recreation	3	2	5	15	22	18	65	3.62

Figure 3-11
Importance of Top Ten Housing Features

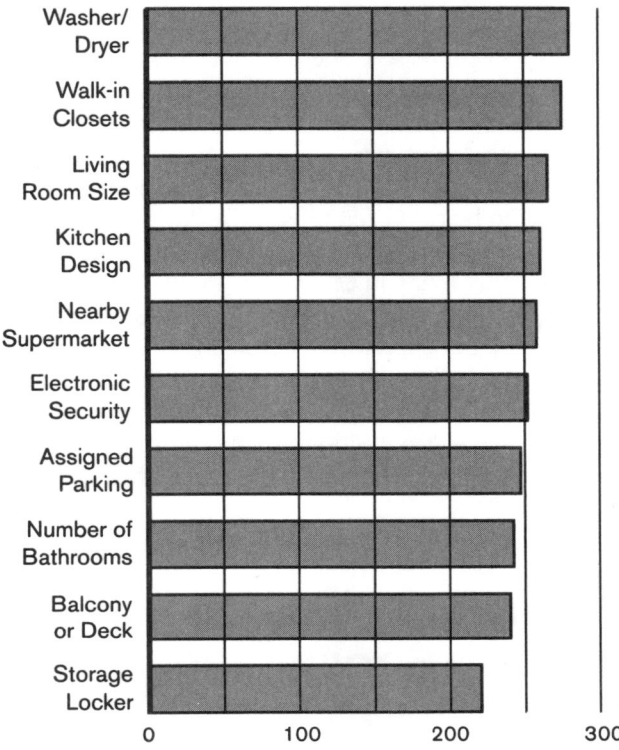

[1]Numbers are the product of multiplying the number of responses by the ranking of 1 to 5 for each feature.

▲ ▲

Household Size and Composition

Among interested respondents, 64 percent would have two adults in the household, 36 percent only one adult. Most new households would have no children in the new unit, only 15 percent would have one child, and 5 percent would have two children. Sixty-one percent would be two-wage-earner households.

Household Income

The two largest income segments represented by interested respondents were households with annual incomes of $25,000 to $40,000 (18.4 percent) and those with incomes over $125,000 (13.5 percent). Forty percent of those responding had household incomes between $40,000 and $80,000 (see Figure 3-12).

These figures suggest that 77 percent of the respondents could theoretically afford the estimated rents and/or mort-

Figure 3-12
Annual Incomes of New City Centre Households

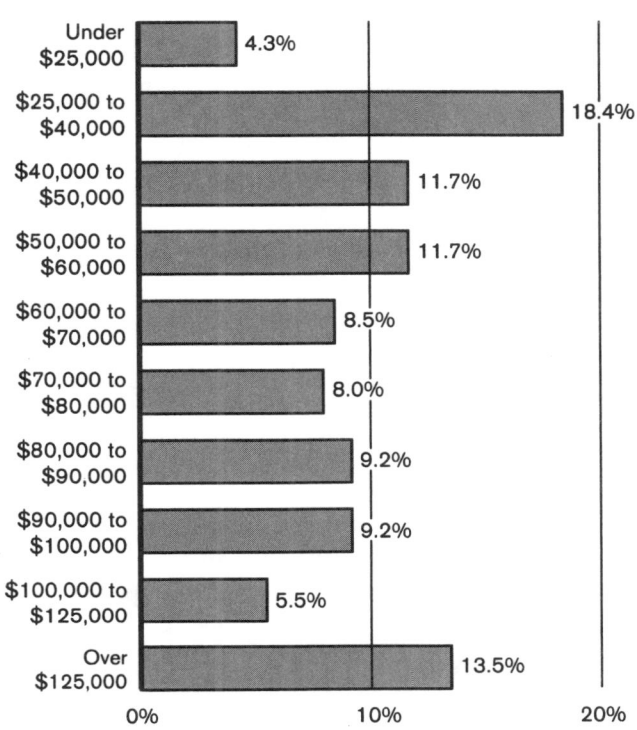

▲ ▲

gages for new downtown housing (assuming housing costs, excluding utilities, of 25 percent or less of gross income). This assumption is based on competitive new construction in the market requiring a monthly mortgage or rent payment of approximately $830 for a two-bedroom, 1.5-bath unit of 900 to 1,200 square feet.

Present Monthly Housing Payment

Fifty percent of the employees responding say their present monthly housing payment is $700 or more (excluding utilities), 22 percent pay over $1,000 per month, and 22 percent pay $500 to $700 per month.

Own versus Rent

Slightly more than 65 percent of those who would consider living in City Centre say they presently rent housing, and another 30 percent own their current home. Five percent listed "other," meaning they live with parents or other relatives.

Figure 3-13
Age of Respondents

	Percent of Total
19 to 26	12.9
27 to 33	16.3
34 to 40	29.2
41 to 47	15.2
48 to 54	9.0
55 to 61	10.7
62 to 68	2.1
69 to 75	2.6
76 to 82	1.0
83 to 89	1.0
Total	100.0
Number of Replies	178

Age and Gender of Respondents

Those aged 34 to 40 account for the greatest percentage (29.2 percent) of respondents, those aged 27 to 33 the second largest segment (16.3 percent), and those aged 41 to 47 the third (15.2 percent) (see Figure 3-13). Approximately 64 percent of all employees responding to the survey are female, 36 percent male.

Occupations and Years in Detroit Area

The occupations of the employees responding to the survey reflect a balance among professional, administrative, and clerical workers and include office manager, secretary, attorney, salesperson, administrative assistant, systems engineer, accountant, consultant, legal secretary, and technical writer. This range demonstrates the potential appeal of downtown housing for several occupational types. Approximately 53 percent of interested respondents have lived in the Detroit area for over 20 years.

Current Address

Survey results indicate a concentration of employees living in zip code 48075 (Southfield below Ten Mile Road and east of Lasher) and 48076 (Southfield north of Ten Mile Road and east of Lasher). Concentrations are also found along the I-696 corridor from Greenfield Road through Farmington Hills to West Bloomfield and extending as far south as Livonia.

Additional Indicators of Interest

An additional question at the end of the survey asked whether employees would like an invitation to visit a new project or to be contacted by a representative. Slightly over 37 percent of the interested respondents indicated that they would like to be contacted and gave phone numbers and addresses. These results are useful as an additional level of screening interested employees who said they would consider buying or renting newly developed housing downtown.

Applying 37 percent (the percentage who said they would like to be contacted to visit the development) to the optimistic potential market pool of employees who would consider living in City Centre (6,200) provides a more realistic estimate of size of the screened potential market. Using this approach, the resulting estimated market is 2,294, which suggests the existence of a demand for City Centre housing (assuming the amenities envisioned in the City Centre Plan are included) greater than currently is being met by the supply of existing housing.

Supply of Higher-Density Housing Serving the City Centre Area

Existing Supply

Over 16,000 units of higher-density housing presently exist within the city of Southfield, all within three miles of City Centre. Residential products range from garden apartments at ten to 12 dwelling units per acre to high-rise towers with densities of approximately 40 dwelling units per acre. Markets served by these existing developments range from dual-income households with no children to retirees.

The distribution of the city's higher-density units resembles a shotgun pattern across the entire area, with existing higher-density units near Northland Center (Southfield Road and Northwestern Highway) and City Centre (Knob-in-the-Woods and 5000 at Town Center).

Ownership of higher-density units is the exception in the Southfield market, representing only about 12 percent of the existing supply. This percentage is at, or slightly above, the norm for communities in Oakland County.

It is clear from the success of existing developments that both the market and the city itself perceive higher-density units as an acceptable form of housing.

Factors Influencing Development of Additional Higher-Density Housing

Presently, Southfield has 1,035 acres of vacant land zoned for residential use. Of this amount, approximately 124 acres are zoned for various types of multifamily housing. Within the City Centre core itself, the only land zoned for multifamily housing is for existing residential projects. Much of the vacant land available for higher-density housing in this area is presently zoned "RC Regional Center," a mixed-use zoning district that could accommodate a variety of residential densities (the 5000 at Town Center residential tower is in this district). The City Centre Plan provides for the addition of some 900 units of higher-density housing in the core area, which would require 20 to 40 acres, depending on the overall density achieved. With the building sites identified in the Plan, some integrated into mixed-use structures along the new gridded streets and some along Evergreen Avenue, adequate land is available. To achieve the final scenario, however, might require redevelopment of some under-used residential and commercial properties.

Absorption of higher-density housing in the Southfield market has averaged 560 units per year over the last three decades. Much of this rapid development and absorption occurred during the 1970s, when available land, financing, and demand combined to produce a development environment that will undoubtedly not be duplicated in Southfield. During the 1980s, annual absorption of multifamily units in the community was just over 200 units, and few permits have been issued in the last two and one-half years. The most recent downturn is attributable to the lack of available financing, increased competition for tenants created by new higher-density products in surrounding communities, especially Farmington Hills, Novi, Troy, and Auburn Hills, and lack of available land for major new projects. Southfield has proven that when the right multifamily product is offered, however, it is positioned well to capture a significant share of the suburban market.

Because of the finite amount of land available for multifamily development in City Centre and the large supply of suburban garden apartments currently offered in the area, City Centre must offer a residential product different from the competition. Higher density by itself is not the answer, but higher-density housing within a special, more urban, and more pedestrian environment offering retail, restaurant, and entertainment uses would be a residential product clearly distinctive in the suburban Detroit market.

This environment does not exist in City Centre today. To create it requires investment in public improvements and private developers willing to provide innovative products to achieve a new vision for suburban downtown living. Absent these investments and visionary efforts, however, private investors are unlikely to put capital at risk for a largely untested higher-density housing product in City Centre.

Land costs in the City Centre area are something of an enigma, given that most developable sites were assumed to be destined for additional office towers and the present oversupply of office space results in a market with few, if any, prospective buyers. Estimates of land value have been as low as $6.00 per square foot, while the last significant land transaction (in 1989) was a site that sold for $13.50 per square foot. A strong probability exists that land can be acquired today at a price that is feasible for higher-density housing, based on a prorated land cost per unit.

More than one experienced multifamily developer in the Southfield/Oakland County market has noted that, while mid- and high-rise construction might command 25 to 35 percent higher rents, development costs can be two to two and one-half times greater, making economic feasibility questionable. The limited elasticity in the local market's rents is an impediment. Though this statement is true for typical suburban multifamily products, its applicability to the market niche contemplated for City Centre is not a given, and only a full market and pro forma analysis can address this issue.

For any higher-density development of significant scale in City Centre, financing is likely to require a developer who has a strong equity position and an institutional partner with access to funds designated for multifamily investment (an insurance pension fund, for example). Traditional lending institutions providing debt capital to a developer with limited equity participation will not be the vehicle for building multifamily housing today in Southfield.

Development Potential And Implementation Strategies for Additional Higher-Density Housing in City Centre

Housing in the City Centre Plan

The City Centre Plan was prepared in 1992 to create a physical and market strategy and design image that would help Southfield realize its concept of the area as its "most important mixed-use activity node . . . a vibrant center of education, commerce, culture, entertainment, and community activity." It was intended to create a modern, functional downtown based on a traditional, pedestrian-scale grid in a suburban community that had no "main street." Southfield's existing Town Center area was a town center in name only. It was a good example of an area of which it is said, "There is no *there* there." By incorporating higher-density housing into the City Centre Plan, the community intends to add activity and a neighborhood component to the area and to increase its population density to a level that can help sustain retail, service, entertainment, and other nonoffice uses. The city's government center is presently located in the core City Centre area, which includes city hall, the community center, a library, and recreation and cultural facilities. Additional housing in City Centre would take advantage of these existing civic and community assets.

Balancing Supply and Demand

The types of higher-density housing that respondents to the employee survey ranked highest are those that are least available in Southfield and its surrounding markets. Other Southfield locations and surrounding suburban markets simply do not offer new, mid- to high-rise rental units with access to cultural/entertainment activities and facilities, recreation facilities, and the public library along with desirable amenities. The lack of such units and the potential market identified in the employee survey suggest that the proposed 900 additional units recommended for the Plan's core area would appear to be reasonable. The housing component cannot be the catalyzing force for the City Centre's development, however. Basic public improvements and public investment must be implemented to encourage private investment.

Target Markets

Based on market research and interviews with local housing developers, Southfield has two potentially promising higher-density markets for housing. First is a market for rehabilitated units for tenants with household incomes of $18,000 to $30,000 per year; however, the existing units and market economics are not present to satisfy this segment in the City Centre area. The second target market is mid- to high-rise rental units designed to appeal to interested and income-qualified City Centre employees, the lead respondents to the employee survey. This market is comprised primarily of young singles and couples and empty nesters with household incomes of $40,000 and above. The survey's indication of low interest in access

to daycare and tot lots but a strong desire for access to cultural and recreation facilities, including a public library, is further evidence supporting the target market for higher-density housing in City Centre.

Housing Products

Based on the findings about potential residents' preferred types of housing and expectations about amenities and features provided, both the housing developer and the city will need to produce supporting and complementing physical improvements if City Centre is to fulfill market expectations for higher-density housing.

Location

Three primary locations appear feasible and consistent with the City Centre Plan. The first is adjacent to the existing 5000 at Town Center residential tower, which might be the logical site for a high-rise structure containing approximately 200 units. Another location, probably best suited for midrise apartments or townhouses, is along the eastern frontage of Evergreen Avenue just south of the civic center complex. The third location, best suited for a new single-use midrise residential structure or housing incorporated into the upper floors of a mixed-use building with retail, office, or service uses at the street level, would face the proposed new east/west street in the core area. Additional residential development has also been proposed as part of the 62-acre Oakland Towne Square. Plans include as many as four 200-unit, 27-story residential towers at the northern portion of the City Centre core area near Northwestern Highway.

Public Policy

To capitalize on the market demand for higher-density housing in City Centre, several public policy issues will have to be addressed. First, the city must recognize that it is no longer in the driver's seat in terms of its competitive position for new multifamily development. Other suburban communities have recently produced more moderate-density (ten to 12 dwelling units per acre) multifamily units than Southfield. To continue to add new units to its residential inventory, Southfield must provide higher-density housing targeting certain socio-economic and lifestyle niches, renovate its existing stock of older apartments, and conserve and attract reinvestment in its single-family residential neighborhoods. The higher-density housing proposed for City Centre will contribute to its competitive edge, but to achieve it, Southfield must allow rezoning that will accommodate the higher-density residences that are envisioned in the Plan. Concern about the aging of existing apartments cannot be solved by closing the door on a different type of multi-family housing designed to serve an entirely different market. On the other hand, the community should adopt a comprehensive housing code with an occupancy permit system as a principal means of ensuring needed reinvestment in the aging multifamily housing.

Preparing the City Centre Plan was, in itself, a major public policy action necessary to help catalyze higher-density housing in City Centre. Now the city needs to proceed with selected public improvements outlined in the Plan that are necessary to induce private investment and ultimately build City Centre and the higher-density housing anticipated. Doing so might include construction of the proposed new east/west street to Oakland Town Square, streetscaping along Central Park Boulevard, creation of the proposed plaza, or other actions that best fit proposed private development plans and the city's resources. Enough public and private improvements must be present in a given location to help produce the environment needed for attractive and appealing higher-density housing in City Centre. Private developers and the city will have to work cooperatively to create the vibrant, mixed-use core that is critical to the success of higher-density housing in the area.

Lessons Learned from Southfield

▼ Opportunities for multifamily housing development, such as those made available in Southfield over the past three decades, do not happen by chance. Early in its history, Southfield made a conscious decision to plan for and to accommodate a variety of types and densities of multifamily housing. The effort has been successful in Southfield because location, quality, densities, and other factors were carefully considered. Thus, solid planning and public policy are important and necessary to any suburban activity center that combines space for employees to live and to work.

▼ Despite its relatively high number and percentage of multifamily units, Southfield has not capitalized on some of the benefits of higher-density housing. No real pedestrian-oriented "town center" offers Southfield residents an area recognized for its interest and vitality. The lesson is that multifamily development itself does not guarantee reduced commuting time or provide the environment necessary for increased mixed-use development and an interesting, vital suburban center. Higher-density housing must be concentrated in a location that is specifically planned for or already exists as the core of such activity.

▼ Even when conventional wisdom based on past practice suggests that demand is greatest for one type of multifamily product, solid market research might reveal other niches that can help a developer or community differentiate its higher-density housing product from the competition.

▼ A relatively untapped market could exist for renovated apartment units at rents targeted to small households with incomes of $18,000 to $30,000 annually. Developers operating in many older suburban communities with apartment projects 25 to 30 years old might be able to capitalize on such opportunities.

Chapter 4

Galleria Area Dallas, Texas

by
G. Ronald Witten

**M/PF Research, Inc.
Dallas, Texas**

The case study of the Galleria area was completed in November 1993.

Introduction

This research, commissioned by ULI, examines future potential for higher-density housing in the Galleria area of North Dallas. Specifically, it evaluates the magnitude of potential demand for higher-density housing in the Galleria area through 2000 and indicates opportunities for and constraints on serving this anticipated demand.

Description of the Study Area

North Dallas's Galleria area is one of three major urban job centers in metropolitan Dallas.[1] This mixed-use neighborhood contains roughly 30 million square feet of commercial/industrial space (about half in mid-/high-rise office towers) and approximately 14,600 residential units (more than two-thirds rental apartments).

The Galleria area generally is perceived as an upscale location, an image that reflects the prestigious nature of most office space in the neighborhood and the high-end goods sold by most of the market's numerous retailers. Further, the small volume of single-family housing in the Galleria area consists mainly of luxury development. Rental apartments in the Galleria area, however, are diverse: recent construction has centered on luxury apartments, but most of the existing apartments were built when this market first emerged in the 1970s. Much of this 1970s-vintage product was allowed to deteriorate significantly when the Dallas apartment market became overbuilt in the mid-1980s.

Content of the Research

To forecast the Galleria area's potential for higher-density housing, key influences shaping its future performance outlook must be examined, including the neighborhood's general character and composition by type of real estate, overall housing market conditions in this neighborhood and market trends now under way, the availability of land, and nonmarket forces that could spur or inhibit demand. These influences on the proposed community's future performance are discussed in the following sections:

▼ The first section examines the current status of the Galleria area and identifies critical trends in that neighborhood. Key factors specifically addressed include land uses in the Galleria area, the market's history of development, the composition of the local employment base, and real estate development trends.

▼ The second section documents the housing market in the Galleria area, identifying the housing base's composition by product and examining housing development trends.

▼ The third section forecasts future housing demand in the Galleria area, highlighting potential apartment absorption through 2000.
▼ The fourth section evaluates the availability of land in the Galleria area, identifying parcels currently undeveloped and assessing longer-term potential for redevelopment.
▼ The fifth section reveals known constraints on the potential for higher-density housing in the Galleria area.
▼ The last section summarizes the study's results.

The Galleria Area: Current Status and Critical Trends

Definition and Description Of the Area

The Galleria, an urban mixed-use development with a regional mall, Westin Hotel, and three office towers, anchors the North Dallas commercial core. Indeed, the intersection of the Dallas North Tollway and the LBJ Freeway (I-635), where the Galleria is located, is North Dallas's "downtown." Along with Las Colinas and downtown Dallas, the North Dallas area represents one of the primary concentrations of employment in the Dallas region.

▼▼▼▼▼▼▼▼▼▼▼▼▼▼▼▼▼▼▼▼▼▼▼▼▼▼▼▼

Figure 4-1
The Galleria Area

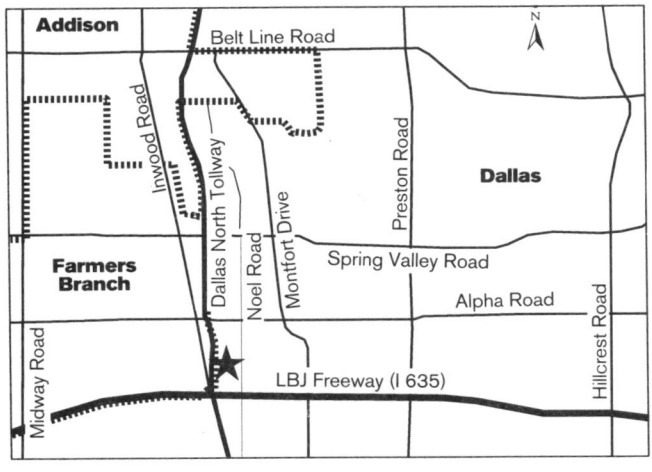

▲▲▲▲▲▲▲▲▲▲▲▲▲▲▲▲▲▲▲▲▲▲▲▲▲▲▲▲

▼▼▼▼▼▼▼▼▼▼▼▼▼▼▼▼▼▼▼▼▼▼▼▼▼▼▼▼▼▼

Figure 4-2
Means of Transportation to Work

	Galleria Area		Dallas Area
	(No.)	(Percent)	(Percent)
Car, Truck, or Van			
Drive Alone	19,592	82.3	77.6
Carpool	2,063	8.7	14.0
Public Transportation			
Bus or Trolley Bus	674	2.8	3.1
Streetcar or Trolley Car	–	–	0.0
Subway or Elevated Rail	–	–	0.0
Railroad	–	–	0.0
Ferryboat	–	–	0.0
Taxicab	30	0.1	0.1
Motorcycle	41	0.2	0.2
Bicycle	23	0.1	0.1
Walk	718	3.0	1.9
Other Means	209	0.9	0.7
Work at Home	460	1.9	2.3
Total	23,810	100.0	100.0

Source: U.S. Bureau of the Census, *Census of Population and Housing,* 1990.

▲▲▲▲▲▲▲▲▲▲▲▲▲▲▲▲▲▲▲▲▲▲▲▲▲▲▲▲

For the immediate purpose of analyzing higher-density housing demand resulting from proximity to this suburban employment center, the "Galleria area" includes that area offering proximity and convenient access to this suburban job base. In effect, the sites located in the Galleria area represent infill sites, adjacent to a major urban job core, albeit not the traditional downtown.

Specifically, the Galleria area includes the LBJ Freeway corridor on the south, the Hillcrest Road corridor on the east, the Belt Line Road corridor on the north, and the Midway Road corridor on the west. The area covers some two miles north to south and three miles east to west. Major north/south traffic arteries include the limited-access Dallas North Tollway, Preston Road, Hillcrest Road, and Midway Road. Major east/west access is provided by the LBJ Freeway, Belt Line Road, and Spring Valley Road. These primary arteries are aligned in an approximate one-mile grid system.

Private autos serve essentially all of the transportation needs of the Galleria area. Bus service by DART (Dallas

Area Rapid Transit) provides access from lower-income neighborhoods in southern areas of Dallas to the lower-skilled service jobs available in the Galleria area. In the long term, the DART light-rail system is planned to serve the Galleria area and to link it to other job centers in the region.

Municipal boundaries happen to divide the Galleria area into three different cities, with the city of Dallas encompassing the eastern one-half of the area and the cities of Addison and Farmers Branch splitting the western half.

Land Uses in the Galleria Area

Primary Land Uses

The Galleria area can be characterized as a relatively high-density mixed-use neighborhood. It contains roughly 30 million square feet of commercial/industrial space, and extensive mid-/high-rise office structures are evident along freeway corridors. Three regional malls plus numerous local retail centers line major thoroughfares, attesting to North Dallas's high disposable income. The western third of the area is predominantly industrial uses, combining warehouse/distribution functions with higher-finish office showrooms and flex space. Hotels have been built adjacent to major office projects and/or along primary traffic arteries.

Housing in the Galleria area is provided primarily by garden-style multifamily properties, with nearly 10,000 rental apartment units and 2,200 + townhouse and condominium units (some owner-occupied, some rented). By contrast, fewer than 2,500 single-family detached houses are found there.

▼▼▼▼▼▼▼▼▼▼▼▼▼▼▼▼▼▼▼▼▼▼▼▼▼▼▼▼

Figure 4-3
Major Existing Land Uses in the Galleria Area (1990)

Housing

Single-Family Houses	2,433 housing units
Attached Housing, 1–4 Units	2,215 housing units
Apartments	9,993 housing units

Commercial

Office	13.94 million square feet
Retail	5.68 million square feet
Industrial	9.31 million square feet
Hotel	3,952 rooms

▲▲▲▲▲▲▲▲▲▲▲▲▲▲▲▲▲▲▲▲▲▲▲▲▲▲▲▲

Relationship of Residential to Nonresidential Uses

Single-family neighborhoods are clustered in the eastern third of the Galleria area and thus are generally isolated from the higher-density uses typical of the study area. This separation helps to explain the fact that these relatively upscale residential areas have remained highly desirable. In effect, jobs and retail uses lie within convenient drives for these homeowners without having commercial traffic or multistory buildings intruding on their single-family neighborhoods.

The study area's apartments are more likely to be adjacent to commercial uses yet clustered into residential enclaves, often with retail/restaurant uses conveniently near.

Development History

Influences on Growth

Because the Galleria area lies in the path of Dallas's relentless northward growth, virtually all development there has occurred since the late 1970s. Initial development pressures resulted simply from the buildout of sites in closer-in locations in North Dallas. This concentric expansion was clearly accelerated, however, by construction of the area's two limited-access thoroughfares.

First, Dallas's circumferential freeway—I-635, the LBJ Freeway—opened across North Dallas in 1967. Then, the Dallas North Tollway—easily the least congested and thus most desirable of Dallas's north/south freeways—opened from LBJ Freeway southward in 1968 and was widened and extended northward to Keller Springs Road in 1987. Extension northward to State Highway 121 (some 12 miles north of the LBJ Freeway) was completed in summer 1994.

In addition to the improved accessibility of the Galleria area, development occurred at a rapid pace (as well as across Dallas) in the late 1970s and early 1980s, a result of unprecedented financing flowing into commercial real estate from thrifts, banks, and life insurance companies.

A more specialized catalyst for growth has been the fact that the town of Addison allows liquor sales (both package sales and liquor by the drink), while Farmers Branch and that portion of the city of Dallas do not. (Private club memberships are required to order alcoholic beverages in restaurants in those locations.) As a result, Addison has experienced much more extensive growth in restaurants of all types and in hotel development than have locations elsewhere throughout North Dallas.

Figure 4-4
Land Uses in the Galleria Area

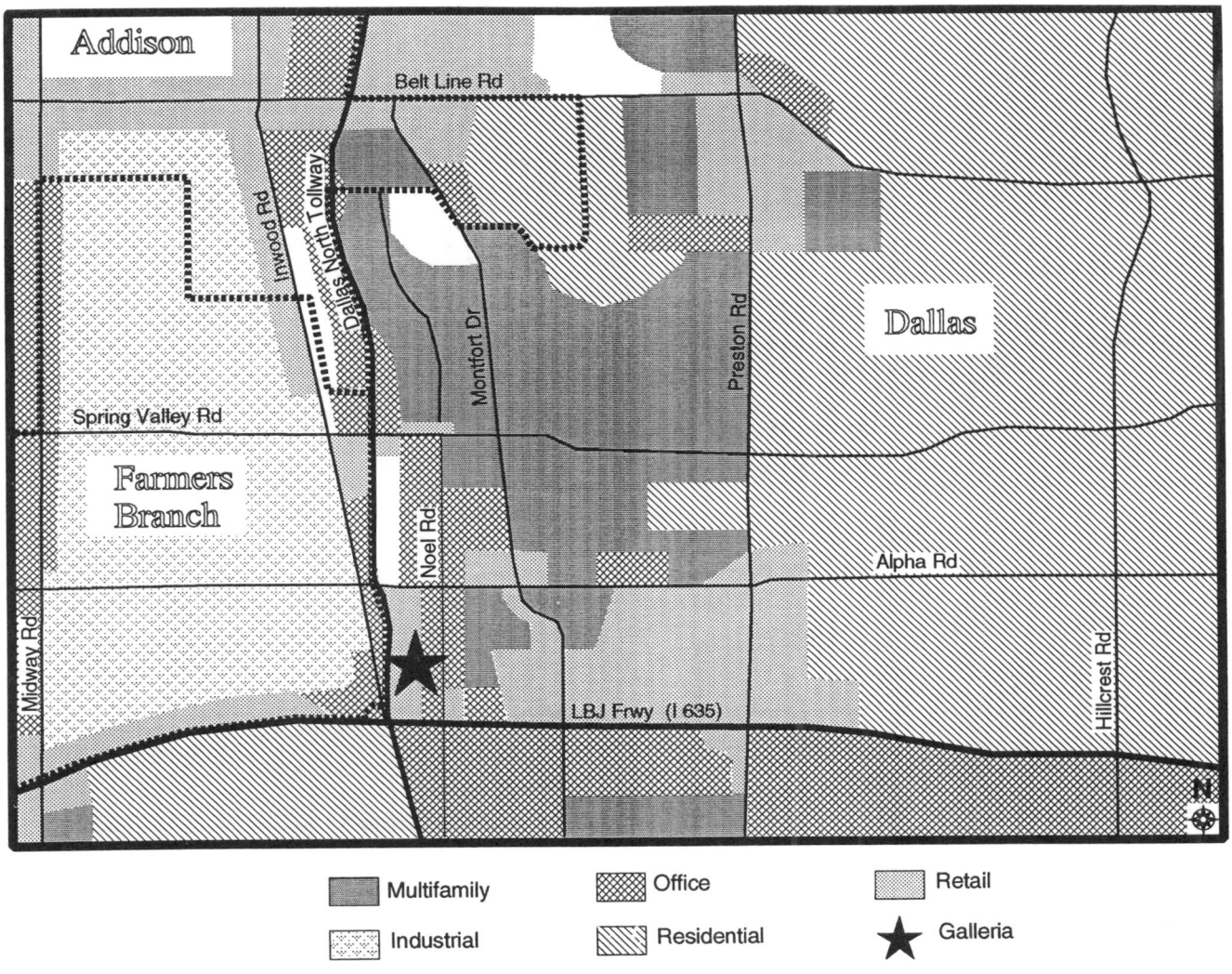

Legend: Multifamily · Office · Retail · Industrial · Residential · ★ Galleria

Evolution of Development

Most of the Galleria area's retail, apartment, and industrial development occurred in the 1970s, with relatively modest expansion evident in the past ten years. The office stock in the Galleria area, however, has expanded dramatically in the past ten years. Because overbuilding ended all office building in the Dallas area by early 1986, virtually all of the Galleria area's office boom occurred in a very short time, between 1983 and 1985.

While occupied office space has doubled in the area in the past ten years, occupied industrial space increased only 21 percent, retail space by 10 percent.

Growth was so rapid and so overtaxed the existing infrastructure (particularly traffic arteries) that the cities of Dallas, Addison, and Farmers Branch undertook a joint planning study for the North Dallas area in 1985. As a result of the study, a transportation management organization and a parking management organization were created. Once the market weakened and new development stopped in 1986/1987, however, these programs were never implemented.

Partially as a result of the problems of the Galleria area's rapid development, the city of Dallas implemented a comprehensive new zoning plan that eliminated previously allowed cumulative zoning[2] and identified corri-

Figure 4-5
Galleria Area Real Estate Stock
(1983 = 100)

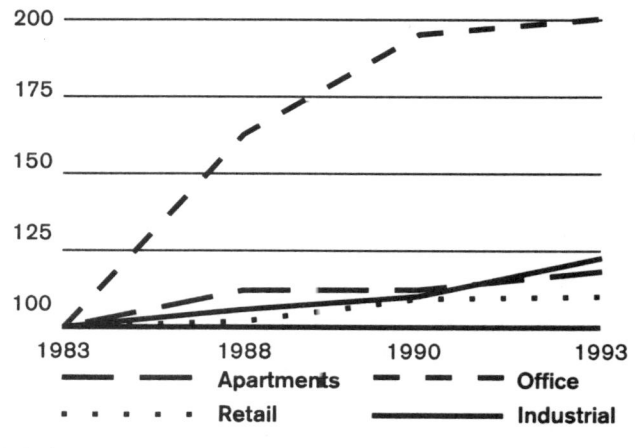

dors where the city sought to encourage commercial/higher-density development. The Galleria area is one such location targeted by the city of Dallas for commercial/higher-density development.

Employment Profile and Trends

Employment Base and Growth In the Galleria Area

As of mid-1993, the six-square-mile Galleria area provided employment for almost 90,000 workers. Office jobs accounted for nearly two-thirds of this employment base, with approximately 15 percent each in retail and industrial jobs.

Thanks primarily to the doubling of office jobs, employment in the Galleria area expanded by almost 5 percent annually over the past ten years. In comparison, employment in the Dallas area grew at an annual rate of 2.3 percent during the same period.

While the bulk of employment is provided by small and medium office tenants, the Galleria area contains a handful of notably large employers, including Occidental Chemical (OxyChem), CompUSA, and AT&T, as well as the hotels, department stores, and auto dealers in the area.

Kinds of Jobs Held by the Galleria Area Labor Force

Office-type jobs are prevalent among the households that live in the Galleria area (but do not necessarily work

Figure 4-6
Major Commercial Projects in the Galleria Area

Name/Address	Size (Square Feet)	Completion Date
Office Buildings		
Spectrum Center 5080 Spectrum Drive	597,100	4/83
Providence Towers 5001 Spring Valley Road	499,700	10/86
One Galleria Tower 13355 Noel Road	467,500	10/82
Two Galleria Tower 13455 Noel Road	423,800	9/85
Oryx Tower 13155 Noel Road	550,000	6/91
Occidental Tower 5005 LBJ Freeway	543,600	6/86
Lincoln Center I	403,300	4/81
Lincoln Center II	585,900	12/82
Lincoln Center III 5400–5430 LBJ Freeway	523,200	4/85
Subtotal	4,594,100	
Retail Development		
Galleria Mall 13355 Noel Road	1,312,500	10/82
Prestonwood Town Center 5301 Belt Line Road	1,112,200	9/79
Valley View Center Northwest Corner of LBJ Freeway/Preston Road	1,673,700	8/73
Subtotal	4,098,400	
Grand Total	8,692,500	

there). The bulk of Galleria area residents hold white-collar positions—in managerial, professional, sales, and administrative occupations—and are employed in the retail trade, finance/insurance/real estate, and business service industries.

Commuting Patterns

Current residents in the Galleria area generally drive no more than 35 minutes to work, and one-half commute

▼▼▼▼▼▼▼▼▼▼▼▼▼▼▼▼▼▼▼▼▼▼▼▼▼▼▼▼▼

Figure 4-7
Employment by Property Type (Midyear)

	1983	1988	1990	1993
Office	28,500	46,300	55,800	57,400
Retail*	11,900	12,400	13,400	13,900
Industrial	11,400	12,000	12,400	13,800
Hotel	3,700	3,800	4,000	4,000
Total	55,500	74,500	85,600	89,100

* Includes restaurants and auto dealers.

▲▲▲▲▲▲▲▲▲▲▲▲▲▲▲▲▲▲▲▲▲▲▲▲▲▲▲▲▲

▼▼▼▼▼▼▼▼▼▼▼▼▼▼▼▼▼▼▼▼▼▼▼▼▼▼▼▼▼

Figure 4-8
Employment Growth Rates per Year

Year	Galleria Area	Dallas Area
1983–1988	6.1%	3.3%
1988–1990	7.2%	2.2%
1990–1993	1.3%	0.8%
1983–1993	4.8%	2.3%

▲▲▲▲▲▲▲▲▲▲▲▲▲▲▲▲▲▲▲▲▲▲▲▲▲▲▲▲▲

20 minutes or fewer each day—shorter commutes than a typical Dallas area resident (60 percent drive over 20 minutes). The relatively shorter commutes of Galleria area residents reflect the abundance of employment opportunities nearby, as well as the convenient access to the rest of the Dallas area afforded by the system of thoroughfares serving North Dallas.

With the proliferation of jobs nearby, the commuting time of the Galleria area labor force essentially remained constant from 1980 to 1990 (averaging 20.4 minutes in 1980 and 20.7 minutes in 1990), while the average commute in the Dallas area climbed by 8 percent (from 22.8 minutes to 24.6 minutes). Thus, the expansion of jobs nearby seemingly allowed Galleria area residents to avoid increased travel time resulting from traffic congestion and additional suburban sprawl.

Trends in New Development

While not near the peak volumes evident in the late 1970s and early 1980s, significant new construction is under way in the Galleria area today. Activity is primarily two types: luxury rental apartments and retail development dominated by large anchors in proven high-traffic locations.

▼▼▼▼▼▼▼▼▼▼▼▼▼▼▼▼▼▼▼▼▼▼▼▼▼▼▼▼▼

Figure 4-9
Employed Persons by Occupation

	Galleria Area (No.)	Galleria Area (Percent)	Dallas Area (Percent)
Managerial and Professional Specialty			
Executive, Administrative, Managerial	5,483	22.7	15.3
Professional Specialty	3,635	15.0	13.9
Technical, Sales, Administrative Support			
Technicians and Related Support	1,091	4.5	4.2
Sales	4,598	19.0	13.6
Administrative Support	4,218	17.4	18.3
Service			
Private Household	150	0.6	0.6
Protective Service	194	0.8	1.4
Service, Except Protective and Household	2,814	11.6	9.8
Farming, Forestry, and Fisheries	54	0.2	1.2
Precision Production, Craft, and Repair	832	3.4	9.7
Operators, Fabricators, Laborers			
Machine Operators, Assemblers, Inspectors	359	1.5	5.3
Transportation and Material Moving	376	1.6	3.3
Handlers, Equipment Cleaners	375	1.6	3.5
Total	24,179	100.0	100.0

Source: U.S. Bureau of the Census, Census of Population and Housing, 1990.

▲▲▲▲▲▲▲▲▲▲▲▲▲▲▲▲▲▲▲▲▲▲▲▲▲▲▲▲▲

While construction of new apartments was limited to one high-density infill project during the late 1980s, new development is more substantial in the early 1990s. Two properties (552 units) were completed in 1992 and early 1993, and another three communities (731 units) are under construction. These luxury units typically feature an exclusive location (such as frontage on a golf course) and/or proximity to employment or retail centers.

Figure 4-10
Employed Persons by Industry Employment

	Galleria Area		Dallas Area
	(No.)	(Percent)	(Percent)
Agriculture, Forestry, and Fisheries	72	0.3	1.3
Mining	368	1.5	1.0
Construction	498	2.1	5.3
Manufacturing			
Nondurable Goods	987	4.1	5.6
Durable Goods	1,493	6.2	11.0
Transportation	1,046	4.3	4.9
Communication and Public Utilities	566	2.3	3.4
Wholesale Trade	1,610	6.7	6.1
Retail Trade	5,083	21.0	17.0
Finance/Insurance/ Real Estate	3,737	15.7	9.8
Business and Repair Services	2,235	9.2	7.3
Personal Services	1,550	6.4	3.5
Entertainment and Recreational Services	393	1.6	1.3
Professional and Related Services			
Health Services	1,091	4.5	6.0
Educational Services	1,013	4.2	6.5
Other Professional and Related Services	2,042	8.5	7.0
Public Administration	335	1.4	3.0
Total	24,179	100.0	100.0

Source: U.S. Bureau of the Census, *Census of Population and Housing,* 1990.

▲ ▲

Driven by consistent double-digit growth in retail spending over the past five years, new retail construction is occurring at high-profile locations (Preston/ Belt Line, Dallas North Tollway/Frankford, Tollway/ Arapaho) or adjacent to proven existing retail centers like the Galleria. Nearly 750,000 square feet was completed in 1991 through 1993. Tenants committed to this new space include such well-known retailers as Circuit City, Office Depot, Sam's Club, K Mart, Albertson's, and Tom Thumb.

Figure 4-11
Travel Time to Work

	Galleria Area		Dallas Area
	(No.)	(Percent)	(Percent)
Work at Home	335	1.8	2.3
Less than 5 Minutes	533	2.8	2.1
5–9 Minutes	2,119	11.1	8.5
10–14 Minutes	3,179	16.6	12.4
15–19 Minutes	3,383	17.7	15.8
20–24 Minutes	3,279	17.1	15.1
25–29 Minutes	1,203	6.3	6.4
30–34 Minutes	2,820	14.7	17.2
35–39 Minutes	383	2.0	3.0
40–44 Minutes	578	3.0	3.6
45–59 Minutes	839	4.4	8.5
60+ Minutes	484	2.5	5.1
Total	19,135	100.0	100.0

Mean Travel Time, 1990	20.7 minutes	24.6 minutes
Mean Travel Time, 1980	20.4 minutes	22.8 minutes

Source: U.S. Bureau of the Census, *Census of Population and Housing,* 1980 and 1990.

▲ ▲

Figure 4-12
Trends in Galleria Area Retail Sales
(Zip Codes 75240, 75244, 75248)

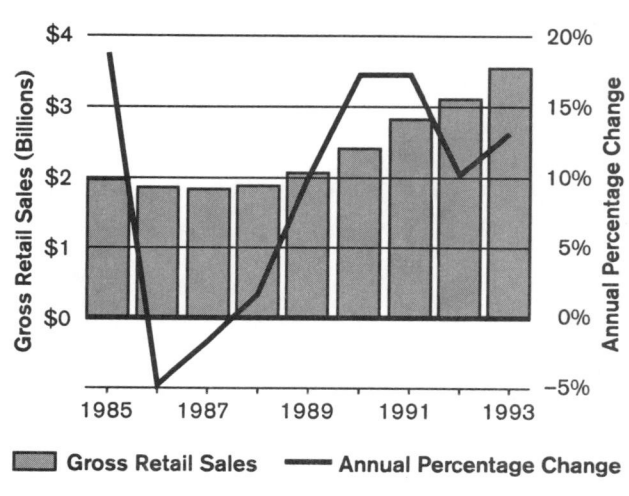

▲ ▲

Figure 4-13
Retail Completions in the Galleria Area

Name/Address	Size (Square Feet)	Completion Date
Circuit City 5959 Alpha Road	31,700	7/91
Container Store 4939 Belt Line Road	15,500	9/91
Office Depot 4949 Belt Line Road	26,000	9/91
Food Lion 18230 Midway Road	32,000	10/91
Food Lion 6921 Frankford Road	38,300	12/91
Computer City 15250 Dallas Parkway North	26,000	6/92
Sam's Club 4150 Belt Line Road	136,000	10/92
Food Lion 8282 Spring Valley Road	36,000	12/92
Frankford Crossing 4625 Frankford Road	93,500	4/93
PetsMart 13656 Preston Road	25,300	8/93
Hi-Lo Auto 8260 Spring Valley Road	10,400	8/93
Eckerd Drugs 6075 Alpha Road	8,900	9/93
Preston/Belt Line 14999 Preston Road	145,900	10/93
K Mart 3730 Belt Line Road	120,000	12/93
Total	745,500	

Figure 4-14
Housing Mix in the Galleria Area (1990)

	Owners		Renters	
	No. of Occupied Units	Percent of All Housing	No. of Occupied Units	Percent of All Housing
Single-Family Detached	2,242	15.3	191	1.3
Attached Housing 1–4 Units	326	2.2	1,889	12.9
5 or more	487	3.3	9,506	64.9
Total = 14,641 units	3,055	21.0	11,586	79.0
Dallas Area Total		55.1		44.9

Source: Calculations by M/PF Research, Inc., based on data from *1990 Census of Population and Housing.*

Figure 4-15
Housing Ages in the Galleria Area (1990)

	No. of Housing Units	Percent of Total	Dallas Area (Percent)
Pre-1960s	143	0.9	24.0
1960s	1,326	8.0	17.3
1970s	7,667	46.4	24.4
Early 1980s	5,858	35.4	19.1
Late 1980s	1,539	9.3	15.2
Total	16,533	100.0	100.0

Source: Calculations by M/PF Research, Inc., based on data from *1990 Census of Population and Housing.*

The Housing Market in The Galleria Area

Almost 80 percent of housing in the Galleria area is occupied by renters, predominantly in garden apartments. Multifamily structures (five or more units) provide two-thirds of the housing found in the area. The large majority (73 percent) of owner-occupied units are single-family houses, although single-family owners account for just 15 percent of the study area's housing stock.

As noted, the bulk of the Galleria area's housing stock was built in the 1970s and early 1980s and is thus somewhat newer than the average Dallas area neighborhood.

Apartments

Currently, apartment occupancy in the study area averages 91 percent, one point below the Dallas area norm. During its initial surge of apartment development in the 1970s, the Galleria area outperformed the Dallas area in average

▼ ▼

Figure 4-16
Apartment Occupancy Rates

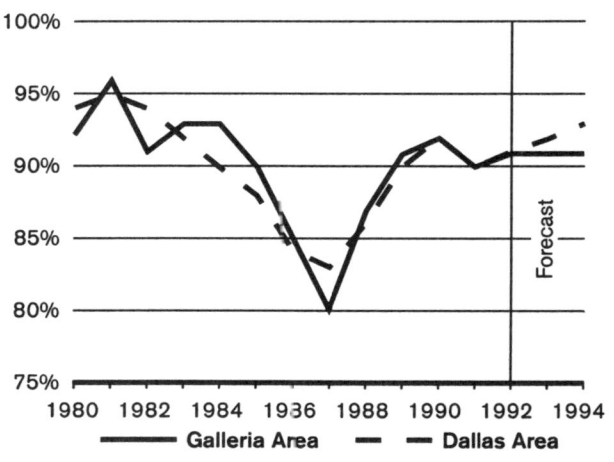

▲ ▲

▼ ▼

Figure 4-17
Apartment Supply and Absorption
In the Galleria Area

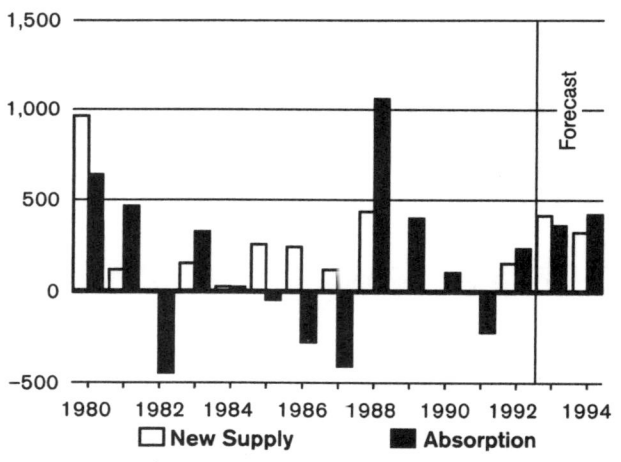

▲ ▲

apartment occupancy, but as its apartment stock has advanced in age, with minimal new development over the past 12 years, the Galleria area market has closely tracked the Dallas area norm since 1980.

With limited available land, apartments in the Galleria area were not intensely overbuilt during the 1980s boom. Nonetheless, vacancy rates did eventually rise as resi-

▼ ▼

Figure 4-18
New Apartments in the Galleria Area

1992	Laguna Terrace	156 units
1993	The Dorchester	396 units
	Jefferson on Montfort	336 units
1994	Carriage Homes at Signature Place	208 units
	Turnberry Isle	187 units

▲ ▲

dents were drawn to the flood of new apartments built in nearby submarkets (especially far North Dallas) in the early and mid-1980s. Even without a supply of attractive, new apartments, though, this submarket has performed near the Dallas norm in occupancy over the past decade because of its desirable location and its expanded job base.

Rental rates have paralleled the regional average, falling during the high vacancies of 1986 to 1988 and since recovering to new highs. In fact, apartment developments in the Galleria area have been able to raise rents slightly faster since 1990 than their counterparts in the metropolitan area. The renewed development that has begun, both in upscale apartments and in retail stores, has drawn new attention to this neighborhood and appears to have led to a rediscovery of the locale as an active, convenient place to live.

As a new cycle of apartment development has begun— luxury infill units rather than conventional suburban products—rental demand for new apartments has been strong. Occupancy among apartments built in the last five years has held in the mid-90s.

Net apartment absorption remained weak in the highly competitive era of 1985 to 1987 but recovered sharply through the late 1980s, despite the fact that few new units were built. In a lull after completion of one 444-unit project in 1988 (The Courts at Preston Oaks), new development began again in the study area with Laguna Terrace in 1992 and The Dorchester in 1993. Another three projects were targeted for delivery in late 1993 or early 1994. The availability of these new upscale units has prompted healthy apartment absorption. Rental demand has exceeded new supply in four of the last five years (the exception being the recessionary 1991)—the first time this positive balance in supply and demand has occurred in the area since the 1970s.

The success of the new product delivered in the study area has generated more interest among developers, translating into more new production in 1993 and 1994. With the projects now identifiable, 1993/1994 was expected to be the most active period of new apartment development in the area since 1980.

Townhouses and Condominiums

Attached for-sale housing (townhouses and condominiums) has played a minor role, even in the urban Galleria area, to date.

During the high-inflation era of the late 1970s and early 1980s, condominiums (primarily garden-style rather than high rise) gained appeal as an affordable, entry-level stepping stone for homeownership. Condominiums developed in the Galleria area featured garden-style buildings (with only one high rise, The Bonaventure) offering flats or townhouses for $50,000 to $90,000. Some 800 multifamily units are still owner-occupied in the Galleria area.

Like other real estate products, however, condominiums became overbuilt in Dallas by the mid-1980s. Condominium prices began to fall as a result, in turn bringing development of new condominiums to a halt. The price slide accelerated in the late 1980s as prices of single-family houses softened to more affordable levels, mortgage rates dropped to near 10 percent, and thus the need to buy condominiums as *the* affordable form of homeownership evaporated.

The result was that attached for-sale housing, which had not been a desired housing option in Dallas before the affordability scare of 1979 to 1983, took on an even greater stigma as undesirable. Today, condominium sales are quite limited in number and are typically characterized by very low prices, with many units bought by investors as rentals.

Townhouses (distinguished from condominiums by their fee-simple ownership) suffered a similar trend in the 1980s. Sales of new townhouses in the Dallas area dropped from 1,006 units in 1984 to only 55 units in 1992. In the Galleria area, sales of new townhouses peaked in 1985 at 14 units. No new townhouses have been built and sold in the area since 1988.

Today and in the near future, attached for-sale housing is unlikely to play a meaningful role in serving the housing needs in Dallas generally and in the Galleria area specifically.

Single-Family Houses

Although dwarfed by the number of apartments in the study area, single-family houses remain essentially the only acceptable choice for homeownership. Because the area is largely built out now except for selected skipped tracts designated for high-intensity uses, only limited construction of new houses is occurring. Consistent with the upscale nature of existing residential neighborhoods (concentrated in the eastern portion of the study area), the new houses offered today are focused on the middle and upper price ranges. New houses are priced from $300,000 to $950,000, on 6,000- to 21,000-square-foot lots.

Existing houses in the Preston to Hillcrest Road corridor command prices of $100,000 to $400,000.

Forecast of Housing Demand in the Galleria Area

In any mature suburban employment center like the Galleria area, available land, zoning, and cost shape the densities and quantities of housing that can be produced. To predict the depth of housing demand in the study area, the framework for what types and volumes of housing can be produced must be understood.

As noted, unimproved sites available in the Galleria area suggest higher-density housing (rather than single-family detached) development because of the nature of their location and surrounding uses, zoning, or cost of the land. Further, because of the scant demand in this market for attached for-sale housing, the bulk of housing demand in the Galleria area will be focused on rental apartments.

The balance of this housing demand forecast thus focuses on the potential demand for rental apartments in the Galleria area through 2000.

Forecast of Apartment Demand

At present, the Galleria area holds roughly 6.4 percent of the Dallas area's 1.4 million jobs. The past decade has seen the Galleria job base expand much more rapidly than the Dallas area's in the aggregate and much more rapidly than the nearby apartment stock. While limited available office space will become a constraint on this growth later in the 1990s, employment in the Galleria area should grow at a rate somewhat more than the Dallas region's average over the balance of this century.

Similarly, the Galleria area has captured 6.4 percent of apartment absorption in the Dallas area since new in-

Figure 4-19
Available Apartments in the Galleria Area (Units per 1,000 Jobs)

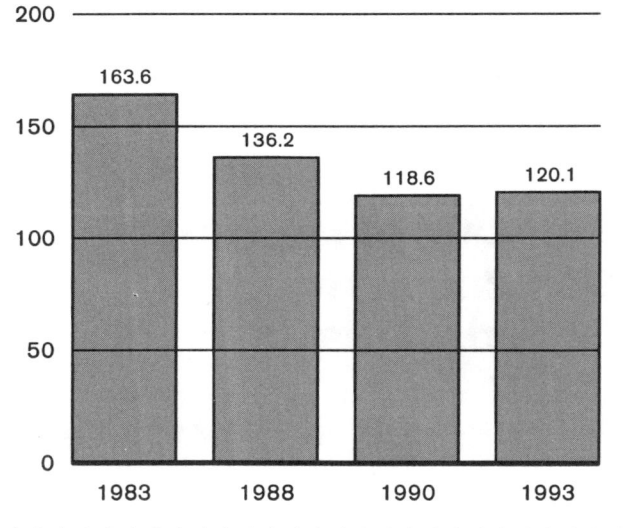

Figure 4-20
Apartment Market Forecast For the Galleria Area

Year-End		
1992	Existing Units	10,306
	Occupied Units	9,378
	Occupancy Rate	91.0%
1993	New Completions	583
	Existing Units	10,889
	Absorption	360
	Occupied Units	9,738
	Occupancy Rate	89.4%
1994	New Completions	544
	Existing Units	11,433
	Absorption	490
	Occupied Units	10,228
	Occupancy Rate	89.5%
1995	New Completions	360
	Existing Units	11,793
	Absorption	504
	Occupied Units	10,732
	Occupancy Rate	91.0%
1996	New Completions	650
	Existing Units	12,443
	Absorption	560
	Occupied Units	11,292
	Occupancy Rate	90.7%
1997	New Completions	600
	Existing Units	13,043
	Absorption	595
	Occupied Units	11,887
	Occupancy Rate	91.1%
1998	New Completions	540
	Existing Units	13,583
	Absorption	567
	Occupied Units	12,454
	Occupancy Rate	91.7%
1999	New Completions	550
	Existing Units	14,133
	Absorption	560
	Occupied Units	13,014
	Occupancy Rate	92.1%
2000	New Completions	560
	Existing Units	14,693
	Absorption	560
	Occupied Units	13,574
	Occupancy Rate	92.4%

fill apartment development began to return to the area in 1988.

By matching or exceeding the regional job growth rate and continuing to experience modest new apartment development, the Galleria area should be capable of capturing 6 to 8 percent of Dallas's future apartment demand. By doing so, the study area could readily generate apartment absorption totaling 470 to 620 units per year, or 3,300 to 4,300 units through the balance of the decade (1994 to 2000).

Contributing to the Galleria area's significant market share are several factors:
1. A sizable job base in the immediate vicinity;
2. Less competition from newly built apartments in nearby far North Dallas than in the 1980s as that submarket moves nearer buildout; and
3. The increasingly strong appeal of an urban lifestyle as seen in Dallas's Oak Lawn/Uptown area, with an extensive range of activities (employment, retailing, restaurants) within a few minutes' drive.

Apartment Development Needed

To accommodate this demand for rental apartments in the Galleria area, substantial quantities of new development will be required. In total, approximately 3,800 new units should be needed between 1994 and 2000, an average of nearly 550 new units per year.

Identification of the Development Site

Aerial photography and physical surveys reveal numerous parcels of undeveloped land remaining in the Galleria area. A substantial share of this acreage is effectively reserved for office development, dictated by high-visibility locations along the heavily traveled Dallas North Tollway, location in a wholly commercial neighborhood, high cost basis in the land, and/or zoning.[3]

Nonetheless, a number of significant development sites for multifamily use remain in the Galleria area. Most of these sites offer attractive settings for multifamily housing in terms of accessibility, visibility, neighboring uses (apartment, retail, garden office, or residential, rather than high-rise office or industrial). In contrast to the level cotton fields that once covered much of North Dallas, a few of these sites also offer interesting terrain and some creekside tree cover.

Development Densities

In general, these sites are zoned to allow for high-density garden apartments accommodating some 35 units per acre. The major exception is the single largest tract (20.6 acres along Southern Boulevard), formerly a high-density office and residential planned unit development that was recently approved to allow multifamily development at an FAR of 1:1. Thus, the site's 900,000 + square feet could be improved with 900,000 square feet of building, and it could theoretically yield over 1,000 units, each averaging 800 square feet. Achieving this density would dictate midrise construction with structured parking. In contrast, the zoning (and land prices) of the remaining sites generally suggest three-story garden apartments. While densities of over 30 units per acre are allowable, current new development in this locale is occurring at densities nearer the mid-20s.

Future Capacity for Multifamily Development

The nine significant tracts of multifamily land identified in Figure 4-21 will accommodate approximately 3,000 housing units at the present zoning. Given the forecast apartment absorption, the Galleria area appears to offer undeveloped sites adequate to serve rental demand for roughly five to six years. With an 18- to 24-month lead time (one year for construction, six to 12 months for project conception, design feasibility, financing, and approvals), a shortage of multifamily sites should become fully evident by 1996 or 1997.

Longer-Term Prospects for Redevelopment

Over time, as the urbanization of the Galleria area continues, further office and other high-density commercial development will occur. In turn, this increased density will tend to create greater locational premiums for housing near this employment center.

When these housing premiums are reflected by sharply higher residential rents, new multifamily development will be economically justified on redeveloped sites—parcels now improved with less dense and less valuable uses (for example, relatively low-density apartments built initially in the early 1970s east of the Galleria and along the Tollway at Verde Valley). Any significant redevelopment of such tracts is unlikely, however, until vacant parcels allowing garden apartment development are built out.

Constraints on the Development Site

Virtually all of the remaining land most suitable for higher-density housing development in the Galleria area lies in the city of Dallas, primarily along Montfort Drive and Noel Road, and secondarily along Preston Road. The city of Addison contains some parcels that would be viable candidates for multifamily development, but they lie well to the west of the study area. The portion of the city of Farmers Branch included in the study area is virtually all industrial or retail in nature and thus does not offer significant near-term potential for housing development. Thus, the question of development constraints regarding higher-density housing in the Galleria area relates largely to the planning, zoning, and land use policies of the city of Dallas.

Utilities and transportation infrastructure in the study area are generally adequate to serve additional multifamily housing development, and attractive sites zoned for multifamily development remain available.

Perhaps the single most important constraint on future development of higher-density housing near the Galleria

Figure 4-21

Potential Sites Zoned for Multifamily Development in the Galleria Area

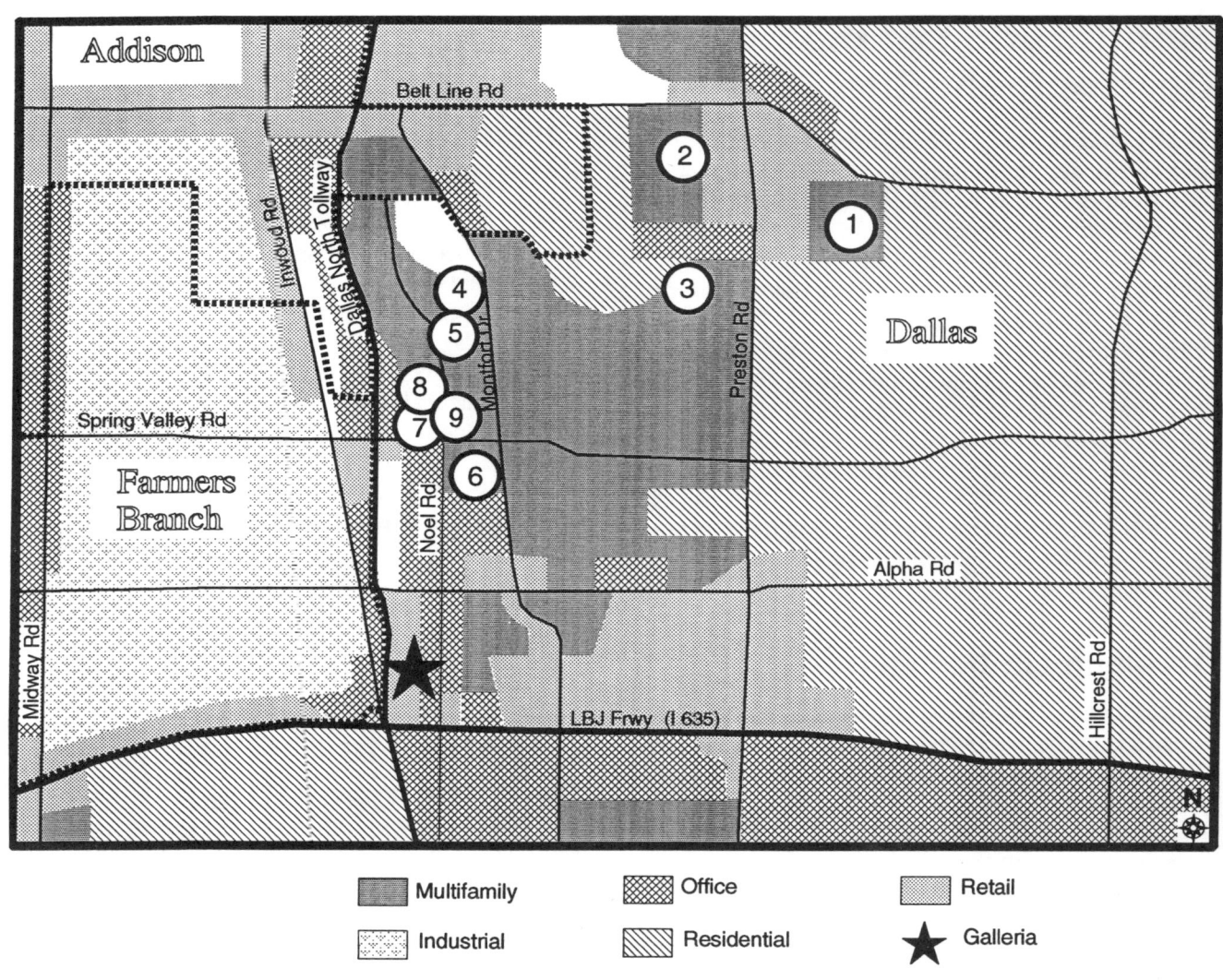

Map Code	Primary Access	Street Frontage	Approximate Acreage	Potential Number of Units
1	Alexis Drive	East side Preston, south side Alexis	9.00	315
2	Signature Place	West of Preston, south of Belt Line	8.17	208
3	Celestial Road	West of Preston, south of Signature Place	9.77	210
4	Montfort Road	South side Celestial, west side Montfort	18.64	550
5		West side Montfort, north side Preston Oaks	11.70	410
6		West side Montfort, north side Southern	20.60	750
7	Noel Road	West side Noel, north of Spring Valley	4.17	150
8		West side Noel, north of Spring Valley	5.99	210
9		East side Noel, north of Spring Valley	6.00	210
		Total	94.05	3,013

Figure 4-22
The Effects of the Standard Affordable Housing Ordinance

Zoning District	Before Standard Affordable Housing Ordinance — Dwelling Units Permitted per Acre	Provisions of Standard Affordable Housing Ordinance	
		Percentage of Standard Affordable Housing Units Provided	Dwelling Units Permitted per Acre
MF-1 (Multifamily)	Approximately 25–30, depending on lot coverage, height restrictions, and setbacks	0	15
		5	16
		10	17
		15	20
		20	30
MF-2 (Multifamily)	Approximately 40, depending on lot coverage, height restrictions, and setbacks	0	20
		5	22
		10	24
		15	30
		20	40
MU-1 (Mixed Use)	25	0	10–20
		20	15–25
MU-2 (Mixed Use)	50–100	0	30–60
		5	33–65
		10	37–70
		15	42–75
		20	50–100

employment center is the passage on May 12, 1993, of the Standard Affordable Housing ordinance by the city of Dallas. This action resulted from litigation brought against the city and the Dallas Housing Authority for discrimination in housing.

This new city ordinance applies only to requests for rezoning seeking multifamily uses and lessens the development densities historically available under each multifamily zoning category. The ordinance offers a density bonus for inclusion of affordable housing units at the site, however. These bonuses can restore densities to the levels previously allowed under any given multifamily zoning category.

The ordinance affects multifamily housing in several ways, as shown in Figure 4-22. Because the Standard Affordable Housing ordinance applies only to rezoning cases, however, apartment development is not likely to be constrained in the Galleria area during the near term, because a number of viable sites already zoned for multifamily use are available. The likely impact of the provisions for standard affordable housing is expected to be felt once the study area matures for redevelopment of existing low-density uses. While difficult to measure, the time frame for widespread redevelopment could be five to ten years.

Summary

This study reveals that:
▼ The employment base in the Galleria area can support additional high-density housing, and such development is, in fact, now occurring.
▼ Existing sites appropriately zoned and located for multifamily development should be able to accommodate this need for high-density housing development through the middle to late 1990s, given the demand anticipated from expected expansion of the job base.
▼ Transportation infrastructure and utilities appear adequate to serve the multifamily development expected in the 1990s.

▼ The city of Dallas's Standard Affordable Housing ordinance is apt to constrain apartment development in the Galleria area after existing sites zoned for multifamily use are developed.

The Galleria area appears capable of producing high-density housing development in the near term without major changes in public policy.

How can future high-density housing development be facilitated? Active government programs do not appear responsible for the multifamily housing being constructed in the Galleria area. Rather, the evidence suggests that the avoidance of government policy has simply allowed development to occur as demand warrants.

Notes

1. Dallas's other major job centers are the central business district, about ten miles south of the Galleria area, and the Las Colinas area, just east of D/FW International Airport and some ten miles west of the Galleria area.

2. Cumulative zoning allowed any use that was defined as less intensive than the maximum allowed under the current zoning designation. For example, SC zoning would have allowed not only shopping center development, but also office development up to 240 feet high or multifamily housing up to 35 units per acre.

3. While rezoning from office to multifamily use has been plausible in the past, rezoning land to multifamily use appears unlikely to significantly enlarge the capacity for apartment development in the near future because of the recently enacted Standard Affordable Housing ordinance.

Chapter 5

▲ ▲ ▲ ▲ ▲ ▲ ▲ ▲ ▲ ▲

South Coast Town Center Orange County, California

by
Richard B. Peiser, Kenneth Beck, Glenn Hickman, and Timothy Siegel

**The Lusk Center for Real Estate Development
University of Southern California
Los Angeles, California**

The case study of South Coast Town Center was completed in January 1994.

Executive Summary

This case study looks at the potential for housing development in and around South Coast Plaza and Town Center, the retail and commercial hub of Orange County, California. The study area straddles the cities of Costa Mesa, where most of the commercial development has occurred and will continue to be centered, and Santa Ana, which provides much of the potential for additional housing development.

Background

Orange County is one of five counties that make up the Los Angeles metropolitan region and is the most intensively developed of the four suburban counties that ring Los Angeles County to the northeast and southwest. Notwithstanding an upscale, high-growth image, Orange County is evolving as a mature suburban community that includes pockets of poverty, overcrowding, and congestion as well as newer planned communities, such as Irvine, for which the county is better known. Large developable sites are becoming more scarce as the area, particularly the cities in the central and northern parts of the county, approaches buildout. Growth in the central and northern parts of the county will come largely through denser development and urban infill, even as Irvine and the cities south of it continue their pattern of large-scale master-planned development.

At the core of the study area lies South Coast Plaza, a super regional shopping center encompassing 2.1 million square feet and five department stores, by far the largest shopping center in Orange County. The adjoining Crystal Court shopping center adds another 685,000 square feet of retail space, including two department stores. The Town Center, a mixed-use office and hotel complex, and the Orange County Performing Arts Center, a 3,500-seat concert hall built during the 1980s, are adjacent to South Coast Plaza. Development of South Coast Town Center was spurred by its proximity to the intersection of two major freeways (the San Diego and the Newport–Costa Mesa Freeways) and to the very affluent and well-established residential communities in Newport Beach, just five miles to the south, the newer planned community of Irvine, immediately to the southeast, and the more densely populated and older neighborhoods in Santa Ana, to the north.

History of Development

From its beginnings as an Indian settlement through its progress as a cattle farm for Spanish missionaries, the area has served diverse users with different demands.

Shortly after the turn of the century, development began to evolve from the agricultural into the urban character that exists today. Early subdivisions and development in the area established patterns of land use that continue to affect development. Large tracts were subdivided into five-acre lots to accommodate a house and a small farm. With further subdivision along a single frontage, lots became unusually deep and narrow, difficult to plan and develop. In the 1970s, consolidation of lots was encouraged to make more efficient parcels that could be more easily developed at higher densities. Two families amassed large farming operations that encompassed land in both Costa Mesa and Santa Ana, and they continue to own major landholdings, which they are developing in phases. The Segerstrom family owns the South Coast Plaza shopping center, the adjoining Crystal Court, and the Town Center project.

Political Environment

The study area's rapid development over the last 20 years has affected its socioeconomic, development, and infrastructure climates, causing political reaction and threatening opportunities for continued commercial and residential development of the area. Development issues are compounded by the jurisdictional boundaries and competing interests of Santa Ana and Costa Mesa, the two cities principally affected. Within Costa Mesa, intensive commercial development takes advantage of the access and visibility provided by the San Diego Freeway. The city of Santa Ana's primary focus has been in redeveloping its historic downtown and developing its own regional shopping center along the Santa Ana Freeway, five miles to the north. Santa Ana supplies much of the higher-density housing and local-serving retail centers near South Coast Town Center.

Mixed-use development in the area has been the subject of controversy. Zoning ordinances have at times discouraged or encouraged mixed use. Most recently, the citizen-sponsored Measure M all but precludes housing development in this part of Costa Mesa, with densities so low that development is not feasible. While a mix of uses has been built within the area, development is usually on superblocks, with a single dominant use on each block. High-density housing has been built, but in large, internally focused projects.

Opportunities for Residential Development

The study area currently includes zoning for low-, medium-, and high-density residential use. Within the overall subcenter, almost all land designated low-density residential (up to eight units per acre) has been developed, the result of several large, single-family tracts developed from the mid-1950s through the 1970s. Designated medium-density residential areas (up to 12 units per acre) are also largely developed, although 53 acres remain undeveloped in the city of Costa Mesa. Under recently adopted zoning regulations, high-density residential development is limited to 20 units per acre, except for density bonuses associated with housing for senior citizens and for households with special requirements.

To mitigate increased traffic generated by new development, the city of Costa Mesa has adopted allowable building intensities for residential, commercial, and industrial development that correlate to a "trip budget." A trip budget is determined by using peak-hour trip rates established in the city's General Plan traffic model and either units per acre for residential use or floor/area ratio (FAR) for commercial and industrial uses.

Potential Demand for Housing at South Coast Town Center

The demand for housing at South Coast Town Center is primarily a function of existing and projected employment. Today, approximately 25,000 to 29,000 people are employed at South Coast Town Center, according to various estimates, and employment is projected to increase to 36,500 workers by 2010. The city of Costa Mesa's General Plan projects employment of 40,800 people in the area at buildout.

Employees working in South Coast Town Center had a median household income in 1989 of $48,750, about 20 percent greater than the median income of the city of Costa Mesa ($40,313). Approximately 25 percent of the employees had incomes between $50,000 and $75,000, 12 percent between $75,000 and $100,000, and nearly 12 percent $100,000 or more.

While an area extending about three miles north and south of South Coast Town Center contains 9.9 percent of Orange County's employment, it contains only about 4.9 percent of the county's housing stock, reflecting the fact that the area is relatively "job rich." At South Coast Town Center, the jobs-per-housing ratio is very high, with 11.75 jobs for every housing unit, reflecting its role as a major employment center. Based on employment alone, South Coast Town Center generates a need for an additional 4,800 housing units between 1990 and 2010. It is unlikely that all of this demand could be satisfied at South Coast Town Center, however, for several reasons. To provide any significant amount of housing, densities and costs would both be high, and both factors will limit the attraction of future residential development. Based on household size and income and market preferences, an estimated 900 to 2,200 additional housing units will be needed in the immediate area by 2010.

Although both the state and the Southern California Association of Governments (SCAG) have policies requiring local governments to allow opportunities for housing, the greatest obstacle in the development of higher-density residential space is the prevailing slow-growth attitude that permeates politics and the populace. The underlying belief is that more growth and density will lead to more traffic and crime, causing Orange County to become like Los Angeles. With the adoption of Measure M in April 1992, a growth management ordinance went into effect that shifts the city's focus from prodevelopment to antitraffic. With the emphasis shifting to traffic mitigation and growth management and the concomitant assessment of more fees on development, costs of housing increase.

When housing costs in the central areas become too high, many people move to outlying regions and opt for a longer commute in search of affordable housing. By alleviating one problem, they contribute to another—congestion. Efforts to control traffic through restrictions on density and impact fees in effect increase regional congestion.

Strategies and Techniques for Increasing Housing in and around South Coast Town Center

The local development community faces a crucial turning point and must try to reverse the current trends embraced by local jurisdictions. One approach could be to use econometric impact analysis to generate and evaluate the economic benefits of continued development versus the negative traffic impacts.

Another possible option, proposed by the city of Costa Mesa in its 1992 General Plan, is to increase housing in the study region by increasing the supply through private redevelopment of already-built properties. The lack of available land for new development in the area and the diminishing cost benefits of building farther and farther away from the subcenter will inevitably lead to redevelopment.

Possibly the most acceptable solution to the problem of new high-density housing in the selected study area is mixed-use development, which is perceived to reduce vehicle trips and emissions, use existing infrastructure more efficiently, and mitigate incompatible land uses.

The creation of a "joint powers–growth management authority," unilaterally representing Costa Mesa's and Santa Ana's goals for development for the study area, is a potential solution to increase housing and promote development in the context of traffic mitigation and other regional problems.

In summary, the demand and need exist for new housing in the area, but its development will depend on a change in the political philosophy of the local jurisdictions, which control land use approvals. The current regulations are too restrictive to facilitate feasible development.

Introduction

South Coast Town Center is the retail and commercial hub of Orange County. It is one of the principal suburban employment centers of the Los Angeles metropolitan area—a region that, along with San Diego, contains more than 12 million people. One would thus expect to find considerable high-density housing in and around the subcenter. The purpose of this study is to evaluate the degree to which South Coast Town Center and surrounding areas have successfully capitalized on the demand for higher-density residential development generated by the high concentration of employment.

Selecting a suitable suburban employment center to study in southern California was not automatic, for at least 19 such nodes have been identified. South Coast Town Center was selected because it is the focus of Orange County, perhaps the wealthiest suburban county in the Los Angeles metropolitan area, an urban center in its own right, and a likely location where high-density housing will be in demand. People should be attracted there not only to be close to work, but also because it is exciting, new, clean, and safe—and close to the largest shopping concentration in southern California as well as a number of urban amenities, such as the performing arts center.

The entire area has been developed over the last 25 years. Many sites remain undeveloped within the boundaries of the Town Center. While some high-density housing exists in the area, it is a surprisingly small amount; most housing around South Coast Town Center is older single-family development.

The following analysis begins by determining the demand for housing generated by employment in the subcenter and then examines the existing housing stock. A primary goal of the study was to determine the *net* demand for housing in South Coast Town Center—how many households would be likely to live there if housing were available. Household income determines what workers can afford to pay for housing. Unfortunately, income data were not available for households by place of work, only by place of residence.

To remedy this deficiency, commuting data recently released by SCAG are used, providing information on where people live who work in South Coast Town Center. Income profiles of the census tracts where workers live are used to estimate the income profile for the workforce at South Coast Plaza.

The case study analyzes the market and opportunities for residential development in and around South Coast Town Center. How much housing currently exists? How much is being planned? What are the impediments to generating more housing? And what public policies would be most successful in helping to create more housing?

The answers have unfolded with surprising clarity. The reason little housing has been built is not just a matter of developers' preferring supposedly more profitable uses like commercial and office buildings. It is a product of slow-growth attitudes, concern about traffic congestion, and problems created by having multiple jurisdictions close to the Town Center. It is also a product of fiscal issues in the post–Proposition 13 era (California's tax revolt), which leads cities to greatly prefer tax-generating commercial development over housing. Furthermore, the public cost associated with housing is recouped through high front-end fees, which significantly raise the price of new houses.

The study is organized into the following sections: a description of the metropolitan and historical context for South Coast Town Center and the surrounding study area; an estimate of potential demand for housing in the study area; an examination of factors that encourage and limit the development of housing, and of the performance of the major complexes in the area; an evaluation of alternative strategies for increasing housing in and around South Coast Town Center; and a conclusion.

Metropolitan and Historical Context

General Description of the Metropolitan Area

The South Coast Town Center is located within the cities of Costa Mesa and Santa Ana, in Orange County, California. The boundaries of the study area are MacArthur Boulevard to the north, Main Street and the Newport–Costa Mesa Freeway (State Route 55) to the east, Baker Street to the south, and Fairview Road to the west. The study area includes approximately a one-mile radius around the Town Center, the Town Center's immediate sphere of influence (see Figures 5-1 and 5-2). Residents within this distance would be more likely to walk to the Town Center or consider some mode of transportation other than private automobile. The Town Center encompasses South Coast Plaza and Crystal Court shopping malls and the adjacent office buildings.[1] The study evaluates all major housing projects in the study area and estimates demand and supply based on an analysis of census tracts bordering the Town Center within a three-mile radius.

South Coast Plaza—a super regional shopping center—and the Segerstrom Town Center—a mixed-use office and hotel project—form the heart of the district, located between Bear Street, Sunflower Avenue, the San Diego Freeway, and the Newport–Costa Mesa Freeway. The study area is surrounded by the communities of Irvine, Newport Beach, Anaheim, Huntington Beach, Garden Grove, Fullerton, Orange, Fountain Valley, Westminster, Laguna Beach, El Toro, Tustin, and Laguna Niguel. Although the city of Irvine borders the Town Center, it is not included as part of the study area because of the barriers formed by the freeway and some industrial land.

Orange County is one of five counties that make up the Los Angeles metropolitan region, adjoining Los Angeles to the north, Riverside and San Bernardino Counties on the east, and San Diego County on the south. The subcenter lies close to the Pacific Ocean and is within six miles of Newport's harbor. The socioeconomic profile, transportation systems, environmental setting, patterns of development, and overall character of the subcenter are influenced by its regional context and proximity to Mexico.

Orange County evolved as a suburb of Los Angeles, with the South Coast Town Center slowly emerging as the commercial hub of Orange County. Over the past half century, Orange County has experienced huge growth spurts, enough to attract major retailers to serve the population and a variety of related businesses that, in turn, have escalated growth, brought in more commercial and industrial employment, and boosted the region to prominence. Overall employment has grown by 3 to 5 percent annually, primarily in the service, retail, and manufacturing sectors. Orange County is nationally known because of the major cultural and entertainment facilities it features, among them Disneyland, Knott's Berry Farm, the California Angels, the Los Angeles Rams, several colleges and universities, performing arts centers, theaters, art galleries, fine restaurants, and shopping malls, including the largest and busiest, South Coast Plaza.

Although much of southern California is renowned for its youthful image, Orange County's populace is more conservative and slightly older, shedding a disdainful eye

Figure 5-1
Cities in Orange County

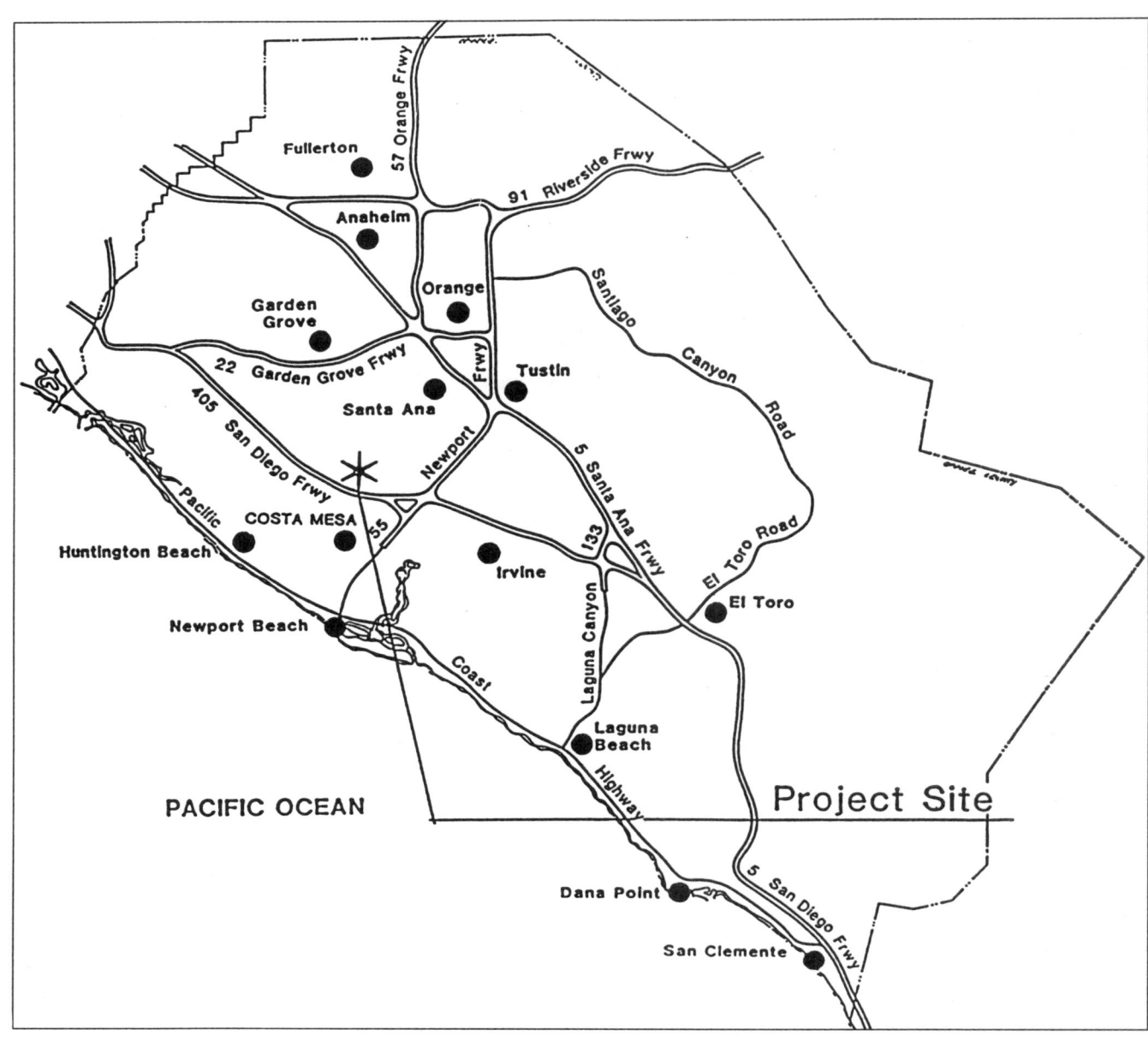

on sharing any of the traits associated with its neighbor to the north, Los Angeles. The area is served by the *Orange County Register,* a worthy competitor to the *Los Angeles Times* among Orange County readers, and it has carved out its own reputation as a placid suburban mix of planned neighborhoods, tract houses, and family values.

Notwithstanding its upscale, youthful image, Orange County includes pockets of poverty, overcrowding, and deteriorating older suburbs. Parts of Anaheim, Santa Ana, and other nearby cities are home to gangs and the full range of problems normally encountered in the inner city.

The region includes partially mountainous terrain on its outskirts, flatlands in the midsection, and rolling hills along the southern coastline. It is served by an expansive freeway system connecting the county to Los Angeles, San Diego, Riverside, and San Bernardino Counties. The subcenter is in the northeast quadrant of the intersection of the I-405 and State Route 55 freeways. I-5, which parallels I-405 approximately five miles north of the subcenter, is a major trucking byway that stretches the length of the state. The other major north/south route, I-405, the San Diego Freeway, is an offshoot of I-5 and closer to the coast. State Route 55, the Newport–Costa Mesa Freeway, runs east and west. The north/south freeways intersect many of the Orange County cities, but access to the east/west freeway is more limited.

Role of the Subcenter in the Metropolitan Economy

South Coast Plaza and the Town Center are the focal points of the subcenter's retail economy. Like many suburban regional shopping centers, a cluster of residential, commercial, and industrial buildings has evolved around South Coast Plaza, many of them depending on the subcenter for their economic existence.

South Coast Plaza, encompassing 2.1 million square feet and five department stores, is by far the largest shopping center in Orange County and one of the largest in the country. The adjoining Crystal Court shopping center adds another 685,000 square feet of retail space, including two department stores. In 1993, taxable sales at the two centers were expected to reach $750 million. Since 1967, when South Coast Plaza opened, sales rose exponentially until the recession of the late 1980s (see Figure 5-3).

Retailing is responsible for a huge influx of visitors from neighboring communities and for the overflow of consumer activity to surrounding commercial enterprises in the metropolitan area. The profitability of the area is further enhanced by performing arts facilities and cultural attractions that draw additional visitors beyond retail shoppers.

The subcenter is the hub of consumer activity in Orange County, one that incorporates a significant amount of offshoot economic activity in the adjacent industrial and business parks. The selected area is a major employer for the region. Its economic influence is a draw to all surrounding communities.

The Area's Character and Development

From its beginnings as an Indian settlement through its progress as a cattle farm for Spanish missionaries and

Figure 5-2
Study Area

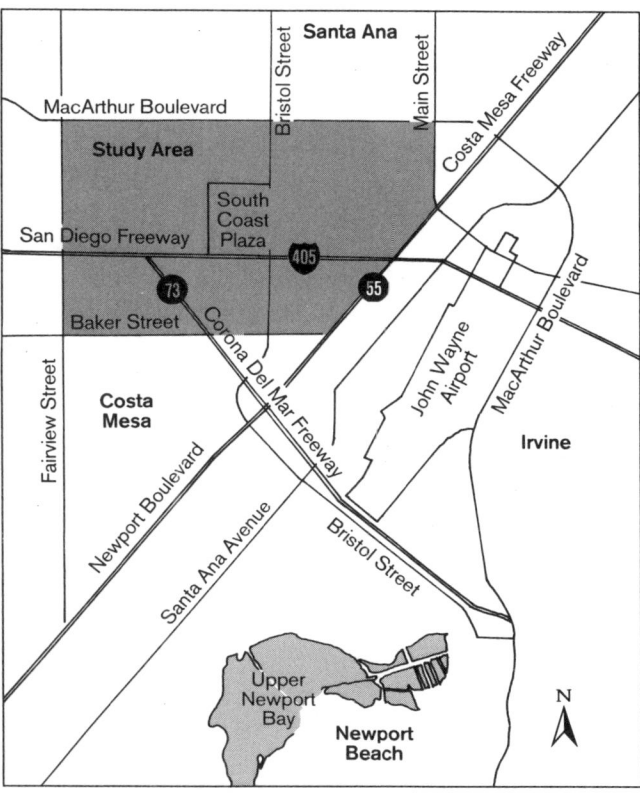

the evolution of three independent farming communities, the area has served diverse users with different demands. Shortly after the turn of the century, development began to evolve into the agricultural and metropolitan character that exists today. This hybrid of uses has shaped present-day development and certainly affects the overall housing and density that now exist.

Mixed-use development originated with the county's most prolific settlers, C.J. Segerstrom and the Sakioka family, who began large farming operations that extended through Costa Mesa and into neighboring Santa Ana. Both families continue to own and farm the remaining land not yet developed. C.J. Segerstrom developed South Coast Plaza, Crystal Court, and the Town Center complex.

The farming community became a catalyst for jobs and housing and, coupled with suburban development, became a metropolitan development. This origin explains the current conflicting nature of the study area in terms of development, land use, zoning, and circulation.

▼ ▼

Figure 5-3
South Coast Plaza Sales (1967 to 1993)

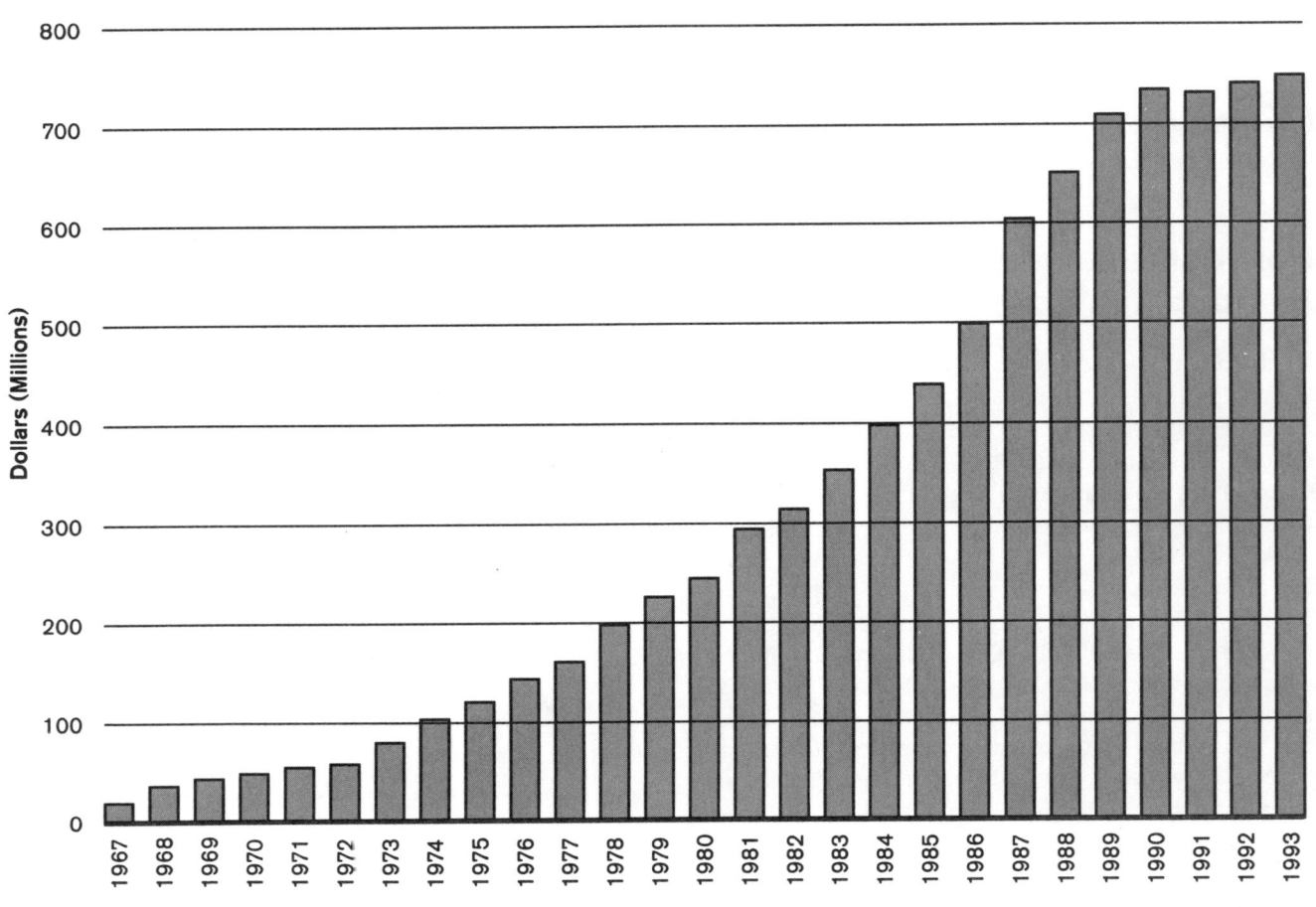

General Description and History of Development in the Case Study Area

The study area's rapid expansion over the last 20 years affects its socioeconomic, development, and infrastructure climates, and poses new and difficult planning questions for the future. Development in the study area has been influenced by the city of Costa Mesa's land use and building codes and, to a lesser degree, by those of the city of Santa Ana. The study area is located primarily in the city of Costa Mesa, with the adjoining residential area to the northeast in the city of Santa Ana. Varying planning and zoning ordinances evolved in Costa Mesa and Santa Ana to provide each community with a balanced mix of land uses to satisfy social and economic needs.

The study area has several different zoning ordinances, incorporating residential, commercial, and industrial uses under several different land use classifications. Residential uses include low, medium, and high density. Commercial designations include "regional commercial," intended to apply to large concentrated shopping centers of regional scale and importance, and "urban center," which allows for intensely developed mixed commercial uses within a very limited geographic area.

Early development in the study area established patterns of land use that affect current development. The physical characteristics of street alignments, lot shapes and sizes, and zoning requirements can be traced to different periods in the subcenter's history. Starting about 1886, large areas were subdivided into five-acre lots to accommodate a house and a small farm. With the introduction of streets, the lots became unusually deep and were subsequently divided again. Once multifamily zoning was approved, those lots continued to be difficult to plan because of their narrowness and depth. The early subdivisions were limited in the use of open space and hampered in overall design and development flexibility. Some of the older commercial lots experienced the same difficulties as the residential ones, and some of them have been combined to facilitate development. In the 1970s, combining lots was introduced to encourage alteration of the old land use patterns, with the expectation that doing so would increase density and make better use of the land.

Mixed-use development in the subcenter has been the subject of controversy. Before 1961, cumulative zoning allowed the uses permitted in more restrictive zones to apply in the less restrictive zone, even if the use was different. Thus, developers could build residential buildings in commercial zones without needing a zoning change. After 1961, however, exclusive zoning was introduced, excluding different uses. By 1974, the Planned Development Ordinance allowed for certain complementary uses to coexist, making it easier for large-scale mixed-use development to be conceived as part of the city's future.

Major Development in the Case Study Area

Over 6.5 million square feet of commercial space has been built in the Town Center, with entitlements for an additional 1 million square feet approved. The subcenter has been an area of diverse and intense commercial and residential development, including C.J. Segerstrom's South Coast Plaza, Crystal Court, and Town Center, and Arnel Development's Metro Pointe, Transpacific Development's South Coast Metro Center, and Regis Development's The Lakes. The Lakes combines 770 dwelling units, two hotels, and a 22,000-square-foot retail commercial center. The residential component, developed by both Regis and Transpacific Development, occupies 47 acres at a density of 44 units per acre. The Lakes was the last major high-density residential project to be built in the study area.

South Coast Plaza accounts for 30 percent or 2.9 million of the city's commercial square footage and 25 percent of the retail sales. The Town Center district contains 20 percent or approximately 2 million square feet of the city's office space. Prospects for intense development continue with the phased expansion of the Town Center, Metro Pointe, and South Coast Metro Center. Sakioka Farms, Lot 1 and Lot 2, consists of 40.3 acres zoned for high-density residential development (25 to 35 dwelling units per acre) and 33 acres zoned for urban center commercial development (0.50 FAR retail, 0.60 FAR office), respectively.

C.J. Segerstrom's Home Ranch is within the city of Costa Mesa, immediately west of the study area, between Fairview and Harbor, Sunflower and the San Diego Freeway. A 102-acre industrial park and medium-density residential project (up to 12 units per acre) is proposed on what is currently used for agriculture and water wells.

Major development is proposed within the city of Santa Ana, adjacent to the northern and eastern boundaries of the study area. MacArthur Place is a proposed 55-acre project to include 4 million square feet of office and retail space and 400 units of multifamily housing. It is located at MacArthur Boulevard, Main Street, and the Newport–Costa Mesa Freeway, east of the study area. One Hutton Center is a 250,000-square-foot, 12-story office building at Main Street and MacArthur Boulevard, east of the study area. C.J. Segerstrom's Armstrong Ranch is a 96-acre project proposed to accommodate 332 single-family units and 448 multifamily units, north of the study area, at MacArthur Boulevard, Alton Avenue, Bear Street, and Greenville Drive. To date, MacArthur Place is entitled with a development agreement, zoning change, and approved environmental impact report (EIR). One Hutton Center and Armstrong Ranch are in the process of preparing EIRs.

Employment

The service sector employs the greatest number of people in the study area, followed by manufacturing and retailing, which closely mirrors countywide employment. South Coast Plaza is the leading retail employer in the area. Major corporate employers in South Coast Town Center (those employing over 100 workers) include:

▼ *Accountants*
   Deloitte & Touche
   KPMG Peat Marwick
   Price Waterhouse
▼ *Attorneys*
   Rutan & Tucker
▼ *Electronics*
   Archive Corporation
   Brunswick Corporation
   Emulex Corporation
   Filenet Corporation
   IBM
▼ *Engineering*
   Emergency Power Engineering, Inc.
▼ *Financial Institutions*
   Bank of America
   National Bank of Southern California

SC Funding
Prudential Real Estate Affiliates
Prudential Home Mortgage
▼ *Health Care*
ICN Pharmaceuticals
▼ *Hotels*
Red Lion Hotel
The Westin South Coast Plaza
▼ *Insurance*
Automobile Club of Southern California (regional
   processing center)
Canadian Indemnity
State Farm Insurance
Transamerica Insurance
Continental Insurance
State Compensation Fund
▼ *Telecommunications*
US Sprint
MCI
▼ *Other*
Los Angeles Times, Orange County Edition
Nissan
Nordstrom (regional headquarters)
Unisys
AIG
U.S. Post Office (regional office)

Land Uses

***Jurisdictional diversity and requirements of the
General Plan.*** The study area falls within the government jurisdictions of the city of Costa Mesa and the
city of Santa Ana. The source of power for these cities
to shape real estate development originates with the
police power to protect the public health, safety, and
welfare of its residents found in the U.S. and state con-
stitutions. Pursuant to state law and common practice,
these two cities are free to enact, within their respective
limits, all ordinances and regulations not in conflict with
general law.

The General Plan is a manifestation of these constitu-
tional powers and, in connection with various ordinances
and codes, is the leading reference empowering local government to shape development. In accord with state law,
both the city of Costa Mesa and the city of Santa Ana are
responsible for adopting, amending, and updating their
respective general plans. The General Plan guides physical development and includes seven specific elements:
land use, circulation, housing, open space, conservation,
noise, and safety.

Specific jurisdictional characteristics and their evolution over time jointly influence the study area. In addition

to the historical development of the area, the differences
in general plans, zoning, and growth management policies account for the study area's diverse land use and
patterns of development. In response to existing uses and
current goals for growth, Costa Mesa has introduced land
use designations to facilitate mixed use and various types
of commercial, residential, and industrial use, although
the residential densities are too low to make development
feasible. Neighboring development in the city of Santa
Ana is characterized primarily by residential uses, taking
advantage of the proximity to employment and comple-
mented to a lesser extent by small-scale commercial and
retail development (see Figure 5-4).

Land uses. The city of Costa Mesa contains 8,094 acres
of land, 93.6 percent of which is developed. Only 2 percent of the 17,577 acres of land in the city of Santa Ana
remains to be developed. Figure 5-5 compares land use
in Costa Mesa, Santa Ana, and the surrounding cities of
Newport Beach, Huntington Beach, Fountain Valley,
and Irvine.

As shown in the figure, Costa Mesa's land uses are
balanced compared to the other major cities in Orange
County. In percentages, it has relatively more commercial
and public land and relatively less residential land. Its
budget for industrial land is average. The city of Costa
Mesa allots almost half of its total land area for residential use (49 percent), the second-lowest percentage of
overall land use for residential components among the
Orange County cities (only Irvine is lower). But Costa
Mesa's 49 percent amounts to only 3,960 acres, while
Irvine's 20 percent totals 5,365 acres.

An unusually high percentage of the city's land is reserved for public uses, primarily because of past government actions. State acquisitions of land in Costa Mesa for
an Army base in World War II and later for a mental
institution have evolved into schools, colleges, fairgrounds,
parks, the city hall, a National Guard Armory, the Fairview
development center, Fairview regional park, and the
Costa Mesa Golf and Country Club.

Fourteen percent of the land is designated for industrial use, including one of Costa Mesa's largest employment districts, the Southwest District. One-fourth of the
city's employees work in the Southwest District manufacturing area, and 41 percent of the manufacturing employers are located there. Another district, close to the
selected area, is referred to as the Airport Industrial Area.
The third is the North Costa Mesa Industrial District. A
remaining 41 acres of industrial land is designated for
light industrial uses and are located in five smaller
pockets in various sections of the city.

Thirteen percent of the land is designated for commercial use. The city underestimated its need for commercial

Figure 5-4
Costa Mesa and Santa Ana Land Use Map

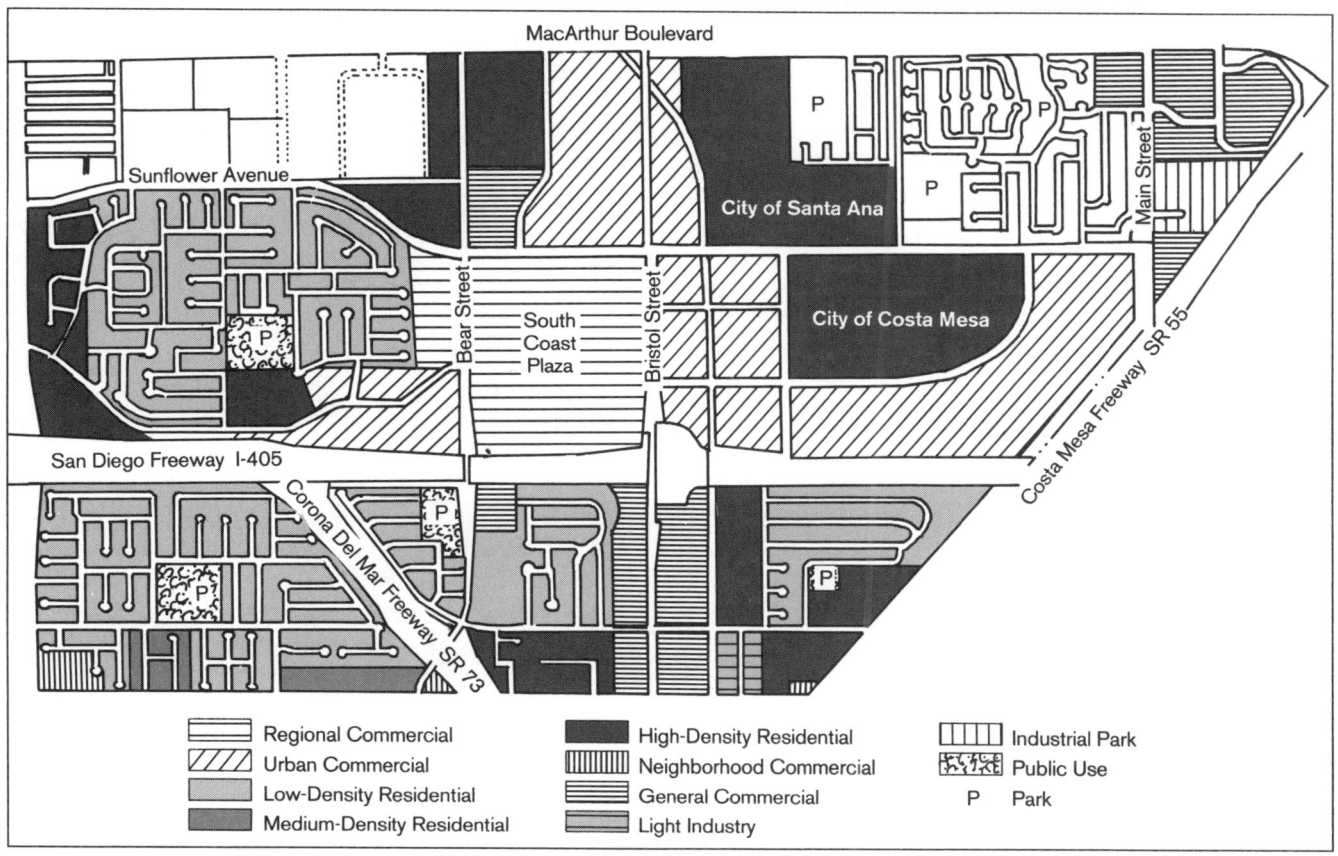

Regional Commercial
Urban Commercial
Low-Density Residential
Medium-Density Residential
High-Density Residential
Neighborhood Commercial
General Commercial
Light Industry
Industrial Park
Public Use
P Park

land and for overall commercial potential. South Coast Plaza contains the largest single concentration of retail uses in the city, accounting for 30 percent of the city's commercial square footage and 25 percent of its retail sales. The adjacent Town Center district contains 20 percent of the city's office space. Golf courses and fairgrounds in Costa Mesa make up 8 percent of the land use.

Land uses in the study area. Figure 5-6 breaks down land uses in the study area. Residential land use accounts for approximately 65 percent of the study area. Low-density and medium-density residential uses occupy approximately 48 percent of the total acreage, while high-density residential use occupies approximately 16 percent. Various types of commercial land use occupy approximately 33 percent of the total area.

The study area currently includes zoning for low-, medium-, and high-density residential use. Within the study area, almost all land designated for low-density residential development (up to eight units per acre) has

been developed, the result of several large, single-family tracts developed from the middle 1950s through the 1970s. Approximately one acre of existing vacant low-density residential land still exists in the city of Costa Mesa, limiting the opportunity for any further low-density residential development.

Designated medium-density residential areas (up to 12 units per acre) are also largely developed, with 53 acres undeveloped in the city of Costa Mesa. Costa Mesa currently promotes density bonuses for housing for senior citizens and households with special requirements, quasi-residential uses, such as convalescent hospitals and group residential houses, and complementary commercial uses within planned development projects.

High-density residential development (up to 20 units per acre) has density bonuses associated with housing for senior citizens and households with special requirements, and it can include complementary commercial uses in a planned development.

Figure 5-5
Land Use Comparison

	Residential (Acres)	Commercial (Acres)	Industrial (Acres)	Public (Acres)	Other (Acres)
Costa Mesa	3,960	1,024	1,164	1,295	652[1]
	49%	13%	14%	16%	8%
Newport Beach	4,539	1,386	302	1,616	–
	58%	18%	4%	21%	–
Huntington Beach	11,630	1,286	1,762	2,109	387[2]
	68%	8%	10%	12%	2%
Fountain Valley[3]	3,345	480	650	–	–
	75%	11%	14%	–	–
Santa Ana	10,023	2,166	3,184	1,626	409
	58%	13%	18%	9%	2%
Irvine	5,365	1,788	3,983	10,905	4,553[4]
	20%	7%	15%	41%	17%

[1]Golf course and fairgrounds.
[2]Planning reserve, planned community, mixed use.
[3]Fountain Valley does not account for public/parkland in its land use elements. In 1980, an estimated 675 acres was quoted for public use.
[4]Includes agricultural land.

Transportation

Overview. Because it is an employment hub, South Coast Town Center draws workers from a wide radius. Some people commute for more than one hour in one direction. Congestion along freeways that feed the subcenter is a critical determinant of whether or not high-density housing will be successful in the study area.

The Newport–Costa Mesa and San Diego Freeways serve as main routes for business and commuter use. The surface streets running through the area are major crosstown thoroughfares used by commuters, workers, visitors, tourists, and through-traffic traveling from one city to the next. These routes are traversed by the city bus lines as well.

The unusual layout of major streets created by subdivision patterns in the late 1880s is one factor that limits the free flow of traffic from one side of town to the other. Many streets east of Newport Boulevard do not align with their westerly extensions.

The implementation of a viable rapid-transit system is under review by SCAG and the Orange County Transportation Commission. A potential location for a transit station in Costa Mesa has been identified near the intersection of Main Street and Sunflower Avenue. An alternative alignment under study would bring the route off Main Street, along Anton Boulevard to Bristol Street, then north to MacArthur Boulevard and back to Main Street in Santa Ana.

Public transportation is provided by the Orange County Transportation Authority. In 1989, the system carried an average daily total of 140,000 passengers. In addition to bus service, the transportation authority offers Neighborhood Dial-A-Ride for elderly (over 65) or handicapped passengers with small buses and vans, 33 park-and-ride facilities, and nearly 20 miles of bikeways in Costa Mesa.

Journey to work. According to the 1991 Transportation Management Association (TMA) efficiency data for County Analysis Areas 41 and 44 and Regional Statistical Areas 41 and 42, 89 percent of all employees working in the subcenter drive alone, 9 percent carpool or vanpool, and 1 percent take public transportation.

Eighteen thousand workers live within 15 miles of South Coast Town Center, but only 8,000 (31 percent) live within five miles, in Costa Mesa, Santa Ana, Irvine, or Fountain Valley. Forty-two percent commute six to 15 miles from the neighboring cities of Tustin, Orange, Anaheim, Garden Grove, Westminster, and Huntington Beach; 16 percent commute 26 miles or more, from Riverside, San Bernardino, Los Angeles, and San Diego Counties. Executives and professionals working at South Coast Town Center are more likely to have a short commute, because many of them live in the coastal cities of Costa Mesa, Irvine, and Newport Beach. While a considerable

Figure 5-6
Land Uses in the Study Area

Land Use	Santa Ana Area (Acres)	Percent of Total	Costa Mesa Area (Acres)	Percent of Total
Low-Density Residential	106		164	
	11		54	
	3		211	
	147			
	267	15	429	25
Medium-Density Residential	15		39	
			53	
			10	
			15	
	15	1	116	7
High-Density Residential	46		84	
	30		16	
	36		18	
			15	
			18	
			26	
	112	6	177	10
Residential and Commercial (Santa Ana Only)	86	5		0
General Commercial	8		9	
	21		63	
			5	
			7	
	29	2	84	5
Regional Commercial (Costa Mesa Only)			101	
			17	
			118	7
Urban Center Commercial (Costa Mesa Only)			84	
			48	
			64	
			41	
			237	14
Park (Open Space)	11		11	
	11		2	
	16		9	
			11	
	39	2	34	2
		31		69
	547		1,194	

Total Area (Excluding Roads): 1,741
Total Area (Including Roads): 1,760

Note: Accuracy is based on maps with a scale of ¾″ = 1,000′. Numbers do not add because of rounding.
Source: Costa Mesa and Santa Ana zoning and land use maps.

amount of housing for moderate-income families is located within 15 miles of the Town Center, secretaries, service people, and other lower-paid employees are more likely to live in Riverside or San Bernardino Counties and therefore are more likely to have a long commute (see Figures 5-7, 5-8, and 5-9).

Interestingly, among all workers living within two miles of South Coast Town Center, a much higher percentage have commutes of 15 minutes or less, compared with residents living five to ten miles away (32.4 percent versus 22.8 percent). These data suggest that additional housing within two miles of South Coast Town Center would reduce overall commuting times and hence aid in congestion management.

Traffic mitigation. To mitigate increased traffic generated by new development, the city of Costa Mesa adopted a system of land use classification that establishes allowable building intensities for each classification. Each land use is associated with standards for traffic generation that are used to compute "trip budgets" for the given use and density. The allowable building intensity in each land use category is determined by peak-hour trip rates and units per acre in residential zones or floor/area ratios in commercial and industrial zones. These factors are combined to establish the trip budget for each site.

For example, the Costa Mesa 1992 General Plan computes residential development as follows:

> The trip budget for each parcel or development shall be calculated on both an A.M. and a P.M. peak-hour basis by multiplying the land area by the maximum units-per-acre standard and by the

▼ ▼

Figure 5-7
Travel Mode for All Residents from Home to Work, Relative to Distance Of Residence from South Coast Town Center

	Distance of Residence from South Coast Town Center		
	Fewer than 2 Miles	2–5 Miles	5–10 Miles
Work at Home	2.55%	2.10%	2.65%
Drive Alone/Motorcycle	76.85%	68.79%	78.59%
Carpool	14.17%	18.78%	12.77%
Public Transportation	2.61%	5.42%	2.17%
Walk/Bicycle/Other	3.82%	4.91%	3.81%

Source: 1990 Census of Population and Housing.

▲ ▲

▼ ▼

Figure 5-8
South Coast Metropolitan Area Journey-to-Work Data

Employees within South Coast Transportation Management Area: 25,550

Method of Commuting	Percent	Number
Drive Alone	89	22,740
Carpool	8	2,044
Vanpool	1	256
Bus	1	256
Motorcycle, Bicycle, Walk	1	256
Distance Traveled		
0–5 Miles	31	7,921
6–15 Miles	42	10,731
16–25 Miles	11	2,811
26+ Miles	16	4,088

Note: Absolute numbers are derived from percentages.
Source: 1991 Transportation Management Association efficiency study.

▲ ▲

A.M. and P.M. peak-hour trip generation rates for the applicable land use classification . . . [see Figure 5-10]. The lowest or more restrictive of these calculations shall apply. Nonresidential uses permitted by the General Plan in residential land use classifications are also subject to the trip budget, and the nonresidential uses may not generate any additional A.M. or P.M. peak-hour vehicle trips than what would occur if the site were developed as a residential use.

Project Lot Area × Units per Acre × A.M. Peak-Trip Rate = A.M. Peak-Trip Budget

Project Lot Area × Units per Acre × P.M. Peak-Trip Rate = P.M. Peak-Trip Budget

The maximum allowable densities in Costa Mesa for residential and commercial development are very low compared to other urban centers (see Figures 5-10 and 5-11). High-density residential zoning at 20 units per acre is far below the 80 to 100-plus units per acre normally found in high-land-value commercial areas. It is even lower than suburban garden apartment densities, which typically range up to 30 units per acre with grade-level parking.

The 1990 General Plan established new limits on FARs for Costa Mesa that are tied to traffic. Floor/area ratios for commercial centers range from 0.25 in high-traffic

Figure 5-9

Travel Time for All Residents from Home to Work, Relative to Distance Of Residence from South Coast Town Center

	Distance of Residence from South Coast Town Center		
	Fewer than 2 Miles	2–5 Miles	5–10 Miles
Work at Home	2.55%	2.10%	2.65%
Commute Fewer than 15 Minutes	32.43%	24.21%	22.78%
Commute 15–29 Minutes	40.42%	40.78%	38.29%
Commute 30–44 Minutes	15.94%	20.72%	22.57%
Commute 45–59 Minutes	4.54%	5.78%	6.86%
Commute 60 Minutes or More	4.13%	6.41%	6.86%

Source: 1990 Census of Population and Housing.

areas to 0.45 in low-traffic areas. "High-traffic areas" are defined as commercial uses with daily trip generation rates over 75 trip ends per 1,000 square feet of floor area, for example, restaurants, convenience markets, service stations, and banks. Regional commercial use is considered a moderate traffic generator and allowed FARs of 0.65 to 0.89.

The Potential Demand For Housing in the Selected Area

The demand for housing is a function of employment and household growth, which are related to population growth. A generally accepted hypothesis is that, for subregions, employment tends to follow the population to the suburbs of major metropolitan areas. After an initial phase in which residential development dominates and transforms the suburban landscape, job-producing land uses follow. At first, jobs are related primarily to producing retail services for the local population; they are followed by employment geared to take advantage of the local labor force, which is willing to work at lower wages in exchange for shorter commutes. Locations along freeways—and particularly the intersection of two freeways—

Figure 5-10

Residential Traffic Generation Standards

Land Use Classification	Maximum Dwelling Units per Acre	A.M. Peak-Trip Rate	P.M. Peak-Trip Rate
Low-Density Residential	8	.75	1.00
Medium-Density Residential	12	.80	1.00
High-Density Residential	20	.53	.67

become the foci of commercial activities of various kinds. Locations near the higher-income housing of executives become particularly advantageous for development of corporate and professional offices. In mature phases of development, which is the case today at South Coast Town Center, commercial activities tend to dominate development, limiting opportunities for additional housing. Whereas in the early phases of development housing grows at a faster rate than jobs, in later phases jobs increase at a faster rate than housing units. Because commercial uses tend to generate higher land values than residential uses, residential development becomes limited to higher-density housing catering to individuals and households of at least moderate incomes.

Figure 5-11

Commercial Use and Traffic Generation Standards

Land Use Classification	Allowable Floor/ Area Ratio	A.M. Peak-Trip Rate (TE/TSF*)	P.M. Peak-Trip Rate (TE/TSF*)
Neighborhood Commercial	0.25 FAR Retail 0.35 FAR Office	1.77	4.18
General Commercial	0.30 FAR Retail 0.40 FAR Office	2.34	3.75
Commercial Center	0.30 FAR Retail 0.45 FAR Office	1.46	3.44
Regional Commercial	0.652/0.890 FAR	.92	3.34
Urban Center Commercial	0.50 FAR Retail 0.60 FAR Office	1.60	1.91

*Trip ends per 1,000 square feet.
Source: Costa Mesa 1992 General Plan.

South Coast Town Center has followed this pattern. Residential development through the 1970s was followed by intensive retail activities and office development in the 1980s. Predominantly single-family development was followed by multifamily housing development. South Coast Town Center, which is near some of the most desirable and affluent communities in Orange County (Newport Beach and Irvine, in particular) and at the intersection of the San Diego and Newport–Costa Mesa Freeways, has attracted hotel, office, and cultural facilities as well as a massive retail agglomeration.

For the most part, people no longer choose to live at South Coast Town Center for the same reasons they did before—it was a lower-cost and tranquil residential community within a reasonable commute of employment opportunities in Los Angeles County. Today people choose to live in the area because it is immediately adjacent to a major employment center, not far from the cleanest beach in southern California and major cultural amenities. They come despite the area's being relatively expensive, highly urbanized, and congested.

As housing development has lagged commercial development in the immediate vicinity, many households, which might otherwise choose to live at South Coast Town Center, have instead chosen to live elsewhere because the housing in the immediate area is either too expensive or does not provide the kind of lifestyle and amenities that workers desire for themselves and their families. As congestion increases and the relative advantages of being closer to work begin to outweigh the costs and other disadvantages, the potential demand for housing at South Coast Town Center increases.

The demand for additional housing at South Coast Town Center is thus largely a function of employment opportunities within the area. Any additional residential development will have to satisfy the needs and desires of the existing and future workers and members of their households.

Existing and Forecast Employment

Approximately 25,000 people are employed at South Coast Town Center, according to the 1990 Census of Population and Housing count of workers employed within Census Tract 63907. Census Tract 63907, while not entirely within the boundaries determined for this study area, contains the major employment centers of South Coast Plaza and Town Center but excludes some office development along Bristol Street south of the San Diego Freeway. The tract also includes some industrial development that lies between South Coast Plaza and the Santa Ana River to the west, an area not included within the study area but one that affects it. Estimates by the Orange County Forecast and Analysis Center, from different sources, indicate employment of 28,915 workers in 1990, about 16 percent greater than the total indicated by the census.

For planning purposes, the Orange County Forecast and Analysis Center has divided the county into a number of community analysis areas (CAAs). Tract 63907 is part of Orange County's CAA 44, which includes the northern parts of Costa Mesa. The southern part of Santa Ana is included in CAA 41. Together, these two areas encompass an area that extends roughly three miles north and south of South Coast Town Center, between the Newport–Costa Mesa Freeway and the Santa Ana River. In 1980, approximately 9.1 percent of the county's employment was contained within these two areas, and by 1990, the county estimated that 9.9 percent of the county's employment was located there. Projections indicate very little employment growth for 1990 through 1995, reflecting the fact that actual job losses have occurred during the last three years. Growth is expected to resume in the mid-1990s, though at a slower rate than in the past.

The county projects that employment in CAAs 41 and 44 will decline as a percentage of the county's total employment, as the area nears buildout. Within South Coast Town Center (Census Tract 63907), employment is projected to increase from 28,900 workers in 1990 to 36,500 by 2010 (see Figure 5-12). Costa Mesa's General Plan projects employment of 40,880 in this tract at buildout.

SCAG provided an estimate of employment by sector, also for 1990, which indicates a lower number of workers than either the census data or the Orange County Forecast and Analysis Center's data, particularly for the census tract. Within Census Tract 63907, the largest employment sectors are services and retail, which is not surprising given the retail and office development prevalent in the area. The tract has a particular concentration of employment in the retail and FIRE (finance/insurance/real estate) sectors and is particularly underrepresented in government and construction employment. Government employment continues to be concentrated in downtown civic center locations, particularly the large government complex in downtown Santa Ana, the Orange County seat (see Figure 5-13).

Household Income of South Coast Town Center Workers

Information about incomes of employees working at South Coast Town Center is not readily available. As

Figure 5-12

Estimated Historic and Projected Employment at South Coast Town Center, CAAs 41 and 44, and Orange County

	1980 Estimate	1985 Estimate	1990 Estimate	1995 Projection	2000 Projection	2005 Projection	2010 Projection
Total Employment							
South Coast Town Center	N/A	N/A	28,915	29,225	32,638	34,015	36,530
CAA 41	55,452	64,308	76,049	76,817	82,127	89,521	96,043
CAA 44	27,965	35,315	52,619	53,150	57,284	59,199	62,206
Orange County Total	915,812	1,045,868	1,301,235	1,319,900	1,557,800	1,730,000	1,885,900
Employment as Percent of County Total							
South Coast Town Center	N/A	N/A	2.22	2.21	2.10	1.97	1.94
CAA 41	6.05	6.15	5.84	5.82	5.27	5.17	5.09
CAA 44	3.05	3.38	4.04	4.03	3.68	3.42	3.30

	1980–85	1985–90	1990–95	1995–2000	2000–05	2005–10
Average Annual Increase (Number)						
South Coast Town Center	N/A	N/A	62	683	275	503
CAA 41	1,771	2,348	154	1,062	1,479	1,304
CAA 44	1,470	3,461	106	827	383	601
Orange County Total	26,011	51,073	3,733	47,580	34,440	31,180
Average Annual Growth Rate (Percent)						
South Coast Town Center	N/A	N/A	0.21	2.23	0.83	1.44
CAA 41	3.01	3.41	0.20	1.35	1.74	1.42
CAA 44	4.78	8.30	0.20	1.51	0.66	1.00
Orange County Total	2.69	4.47	0.29	3.37	2.12	1.74

Sources: 1980 estimates are from Orange County Preferred Projections 1985 (OCP-85); 1985 estimates are interpolated from OCP-88 modified; 1990 estimates and forecasts are from OCP-92 modified.

a way of estimating household income, data were obtained that identified workers at South Coast Town Center by place of residence. Workers living in each tract were assumed to share the income distribution of the entire tract, except that the two lowest income categories (those with incomes below $10,000 per year) were not included.

Employees working within South Coast Town Center are estimated to have had a median household income in 1989 of $48,750, about 20 percent greater than the median income of the city of Costa Mesa ($40,313). Approximately 25 percent of the employees had incomes between $50,000 and $75,000, 12 percent between $75,000 and $100,000, and nearly 12 percent $100,000 or more.

Distance of Residence from Workplace

Based on an analysis of data from the 1990 Census of Population and Housing, more than one-third of the workers employed at South Coast Town Center (Census Tract 63907) live within five miles of their place of work, and nearly two-thirds live within ten miles (see Figure 5-14).

Figure 5-15 presents an estimate of the income distribution of workers at South Coast Town Center by distance of residence from the Town Center. The comparison shows incomes of workers who live close to South Coast Town Center do not vary widely from those who live farther away. In particular, the incomes of those who live more

Figure 5-13

Estimated Employment by Sector at South Coast Town Center, Adjoining CAAs, and Orange County

	South Coast Town Center (Census Tract 63907)		CAA 44 (Northern Costa Mesa)*		CAA 41 (Southern Santa Ana)		Total CAA 41 and CAA 44		Orange County Total	
Agriculture	17	0%	243	0%	609	1%	852	1%	6,897	1%
Mining	0	0%	22	0%	41	0%	63	0%	1,391	0%
Construction	220	1%	1,737	3%	3,666	5%	5,403	4%	62,597	5%
Manufacturing	3,926	18%	6,703	13%	28,742	41%	35,445	29%	254,686	20%
Utilities	212	1%	797	2%	1,363	2%	2,160	2%	38,615	3%
Wholesale Trade	1,457	7%	2,856	6%	7,024	10%	9,880	8%	88,110	7%
Retail Trade	6,248	29%	11,657	23%	7,946	11%	19,603	16%	225,603	17%
FIRE	2,314	11%	6,187	12%	1,513	2%	7,700	6%	105,710	8%
Services	7,459	34%	21,378	41%	18,662	27%	40,040	33%	460,394	35%
Government	16	0%	216	0%	778	1%	994	1%	61,081	5%
Total	21,869		51,796		70,344		122,140		1,305,084	

*Includes Census Tract 63907.
Source: Southern California Association of Governments.

than ten miles from South Coast Town Center have characteristics very similar to those of all workers within the area. The greatest differences are that a relatively higher concentration of low-income workers lives two to five miles from South Coast Town Center (which includes

Figure 5-14

Distance of Residence to Work for Workers Employed at South Coast Town Center*

	Number of Workers	Percent of Total
Fewer than 2 Miles	1,869	7.63
2–5 Miles	6,901	28.18
5–10 Miles	7,050	28.79
More than 10 Miles	8,666	35.39
Total	24,486	100.00

*Based on all workers employed within Census Tract 63907.
Source: 1990 Census Transportation Data Series.

lower-income areas of Santa Ana) and higher-income workers living within two miles of South Coast Town Center are underrepresented. Although an estimated 3.9 percent of the workers at South Coast Town Center have household incomes of $150,000 or more, only about 1.5 percent of workers living within two miles are estimated to have incomes in that range. The nicest housing, along the ocean in Newport Beach, is five to seven miles away.

Historic and Projected Household Growth

While CAA 41 and CAA 44 contain about 9.9 percent of Orange County's employment, they contain only about 4.9 percent of the county's housing stock. This share has declined from 5.3 percent in 1980, and it is projected to continue to decline between 1990 and 2010, reflecting the relatively built-out condition of the area (see Figure 5-16). Between 1990 and 2010, the county projects that 1,250 additional housing units will be added to the existing stock at South Coast Town Center, nearly a 50 percent increase over the 2,461 in place in 1990.

Figure 5-15
Income Distribution of Workers at South Coast Town Center by Distance of Residence from South Coast Town Center

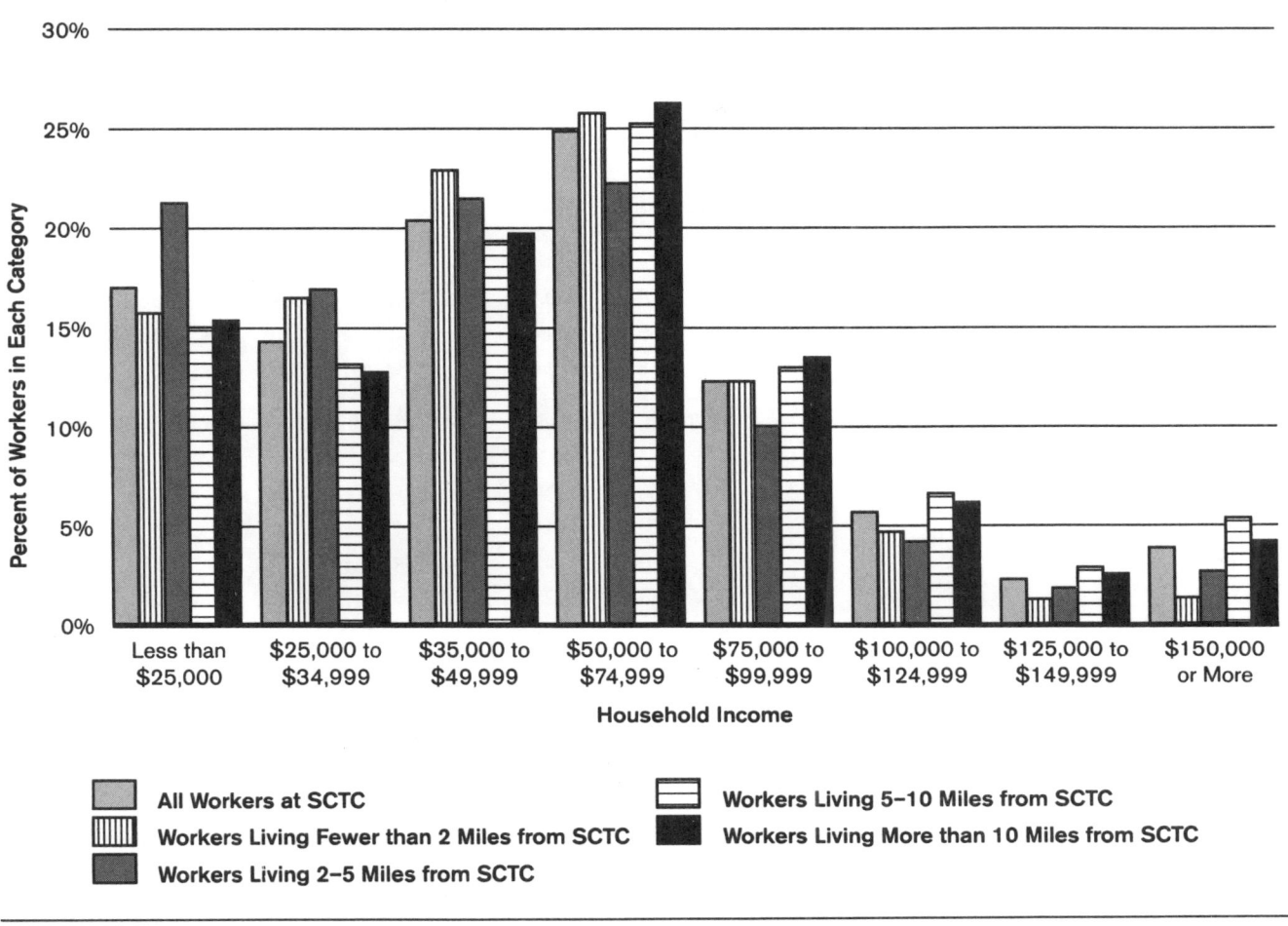

Household Income

Legend:
- All Workers at SCTC
- Workers Living Fewer than 2 Miles from SCTC
- Workers Living 2–5 Miles from SCTC
- Workers Living 5–10 Miles from SCTC
- Workers Living More than 10 Miles from SCTC

Source: 1990 Census of Population and Housing.

In 1990, 53,690 residents lived within two miles of South Coast Town Center, 433,396 lived from two to five miles away, and 784,506 lived from five to ten miles away. The average household size was about 2.9 persons (see Figure 5-17).

Homeownership

Within South Coast Town Center, 44 percent of the households are owner-occupants, 56 percent renters. Homeownership rates tend to increase as the distance from South Coast Town Center increases. In the area five to ten miles away, 59 percent of all households are homeowners (see Figure 5-18).

Jobs-per-Housing Ratio

The ratio between the number of jobs and housing units in an area, compared to a similar ratio for the entire county or region, is a useful indicator of the relative balance of land uses within the area. An area with a ratio higher than the county's or region's is relatively "job rich"; an area with a ratio lower than the county's or region's is relatively "housing rich" or "job poor," depending on the point of view. Orange County in 1980 had 1.27 jobs for every housing unit; by 1990, that ratio had increased to 1.49. In part, the increase reflects increased participation in the labor force, but largely it reflects Orange County's becoming job rich relative to the region. Increasingly,

Figure 5-16

Estimated Historic and Projected Housing at South Coast Town Center, CAAs 41 and 44, and Orange County

	1980 Estimate	1985 Estimate	1990 Estimate	1995 Projection	2000 Projection	2005 Projection	2010 Projection
Housing Units							
South Coast Town Center	N/A	N/A	2,461	3,108	3,552	3,641	3,718
CAA 41	20,285	20,911	21,439	21,773	21,903	22,329	22,756
CAA 44	17,906	19,202	21,814	23,286	24,050	24,235	24,419
Orange County Total	721,514	788,853	875,105	934,000	1,004,800	1,051,600	1,092,200
Housing as Percent of County Total							
South Coast Town Center	N/A	N/A	0.28	0.33	0.35	0.35	0.34
CAA 41	2.81	2.65	2.45	2.33	2.18	2.12	2.08
CAA 44	2.48	2.43	2.49	2.49	2.39	2.30	2.24

	1980–85	1985–90	1990–95	1995–2000	2000–05	2005–10
Average Annual Increase (Number)						
South Coast Town Center	N/A	N/A	129	89	18	15
CAA 41	125	106	67	26	85	85
CAA 44	259	522	294	153	37	37
Orange County Total	13,468	17,250	11,779	14,160	9,360	8,120
Average Annual Growth Rate (Percent)						
South Coast Town Center	N/A	N/A	4.78	2.71	0.50	0.42
CAA 41	0.61	0.50	0.31	0.12	0.39	0.38
CAA 44	1.41	2.58	1.31	0.65	0.15	0.15
Orange County Total	1.80	2.10	1.31	1.47	0.91	0.76

Sources: 1980 estimates are from Orange County Preferred Projections 1985 (OCP-85); 1985 estimates are interpolated from OCP-88 modified; 1990 estimates and forecasts are from OCP-92 modified.

workers commute to jobs in Orange County from surrounding counties. The county projects that this ratio, after a decline from 1990 to 1995 (primarily as a result of job losses in the current recession), will continue to rise for the county as a whole, reaching 1.73 in 2010. By comparison, SCAG projects that for the region, the jobs-per-housing ratio will decline to 1.22 as a result of an aging population and decreasing participation in the labor force.

Both CAA 41 and CAA 44 are job rich, with 3.55 and 2.41 jobs for every housing unit, respectively. Taken together, these two areas have one-half the housing units they would have if the jobs-per-housing ratio matched that of the county as a whole. At South Coast Town Center, the ratio is very high, with 11.75 jobs for every hous-

ing unit, reflecting its role as a major employment center. Even with the additional housing units projected by the county, the ratio is projected to remain considerably higher for South Coast Town Center than for the county as a whole or the remainder of CAAs 41 and 44 (see Figure 5-19).

Potential Demand

The potential demand for housing at South Coast Town Center as a function of employment might be estimated as that that would bring a jobs-per-housing balance to the area. It would not be realistic to expect that all of that demand would be accommodated within the Town

Figure 5-17
Population, Households, Density, and Income
In and around South Coast Town Center

		Distance of Residence from South Coast Town Center		
	Census Tract 63907	Fewer than 2 Miles*	2–5 Miles	5–10 Miles
Population	5,069	53,690	433,396	784,506
Households	2,283	18,592	129,374	270,893
Persons per Household	2.22	2.89	3.35	2.90
Households per Square Mile	N/A	1,480	1,961	1,150
Average Median Income**	$50,781	$44,595	$43,363	$48,142

*Includes Census Tract 63907.
**Average median income was determined by dividing the product of the median household income for each census tract and the number of households in each tract by the total number of households in the area.
Source: 1990 Census of Population and Housing.

Figure 5-18
Percentage of Owner-Occupied and Renter Households Relative to
Distance of Residence from South Coast Town Center

		Distance of Residence from South Coast Town Center		
	Census Tract 63907	Fewer than 2 Miles	2–5 Miles	5–10 Miles
Owner-Occupied Households (Percent)	44.14	48.85	50.43	59.17
Renter Households (Percent)	55.86	51.15	49.57	40.83

Source: 1990 Census of Housing and Population.

Center itself, but it might be reasonable to expect that CAAs 41 and 44 would achieve the same balance as the county as a whole and that South Coast Town Center would provide the same percentage of housing within these two analysis areas as is currently the case and projected by county planners. Today, 43,253 housing units exist in CAAs 41 and 44, 2,461 of which (5.69 percent) are within South Coast Town Center and the adjoining neighborhoods making up the study area.

Given that CAAs 41 and 44 have only half the housing that would exist if the areas matched the county's jobs-per-housing ratio, it can be estimated that South Coast Town Center's share of that currently unmet demand would roughly equal its current housing stock. Between now and 2010, a total of 4,762 housing units could be added to South Coast Town Center, based on correcting the current jobs-per-housing imbalance in the area plus

providing for the households of future workers (see Figure 5-20).

It is unlikely, however, that all of this demand could be satisfied at South Coast Town Center for several reasons. To provide any significant amount of housing, densities and housing costs will both be high, and both factors would limit the ability of future residential development to attract residents from the full spectrum of households.

Higher-density housing in Orange County is likely to appeal primarily to one- and two-person households of all age groups. Roughly one-half of the households living within ten miles of South Coast Town Center consist of one or two persons. At South Coast Town Center, the percentage is higher—65 percent of all households (see Figure 5-21). Relatively small, high-density housing units are likely to appeal to no more than one-half the potential market, based on household size and lifestyle alone.

Figure 5-19
Estimated Historic and Projected Jobs-per-Housing Ratios for South Coast Town Center, CAAs 41 and 44, and Orange County

	1980 Estimate	1985 Estimate	1990 Estimate	1995 Projection	2000 Projection	2005 Projection	2010 Projection
Jobs-per-Housing Ratio							
South Coast Town Center	N/A	N/A	11.75	9.40	9.19	9.34	9.83
CAA 41	2.73	3.08	3.55	3.53	3.75	4.01	4.22
CAA 44	1.56	1.84	2.41	2.28	2.38	2.44	2.55
Orange County Total	1.27	1.33	1.49	1.41	1.55	1.65	1.73
Job-per-Housing Ratio Compared to County							
South Coast Town Center	N/A	N/A	7.90	6.65	5.93	5.68	5.69
CAA 41	2.15	2.32	2.39	2.50	2.42	2.44	2.44
CAA 44	1.23	1.39	1.62	1.62	1.54	1.48	1.48

Sources: 1980 estimates are from Orange County Preferred Projections 1985 (OCP-85); 1985 estimates are interpolated from OCP-88 modified; 1990 estimates and forecasts are from OCP-92 modified.

High rents and sale prices will be the result both of greater construction costs associated with high-density housing and greater land values resulting from the need to compete with commercial uses. The high rents and prices needed to make housing feasible will limit the size of the market.

Income and Affordable Housing

A direct relationship exists between household income and the ability to afford housing. Figure 5-22 shows the maximum monthly rent that could be paid for various income ranges and the percentage of workers at South Coast Town Center that fall within each range. For apartments, the calculation assumes that rent will not exceed 30 percent of income. For example, a household with an income of $37,500 to $39,999 could afford to pay no more than $969 per month on rent. (In the table, the midpoint of each range is used, except for the top and bottom categories. For the bottom category, the upper end of the range is used; for the top category, an annual income of $200,000 is assumed.)

For owned housing, mortgage payments were assumed not to exceed 25 percent of household income. (The lower percentage makes allowance for taxes, insurance, and association dues, which, when factored in, bring the total housing cost to approximately 30 percent of income.) Further, it was assumed that the household could

afford an initial 20 percent downpayment and that an 8 percent, 30-year mortgage could be obtained for the remainder. With these assumptions, a household can afford to purchase a house with a price about 3.5 times annual income. For example, a household earning $37,500 to $39,999 could afford to pay no more than $137,500 for a house.

Based on these assumptions, a household with the median household income of workers at South Coast Town Center ($48,750) could afford to pay $1,200 per month in rent or purchase a house for $173,000. About 40 percent of the households working at South Coast Town Center could afford to pay $200,000 or more for a house, and 9 percent could afford to pay $300,000 or more.

With a 10 percent downpayment, the maximum price a household could afford would be reduced about 11 percent. Similarly, a household that could afford a larger downpayment could afford to pay more. For higher-priced houses particularly, household wealth might be as important as, or more important than, income in determining affordability.

Land Value and Feasibility of Development

Whether ownership (condominium) or rental (apartment) housing is built, the prices and rents will have to be at a level that is sufficient to support the feasibility of develop-

Figure 5-20

Estimated Unmet and Total Potential Demand for Additional Housing Units at South Coast Town Center (Based on the County Jobs-per-Housing Ratio)

	1990	1995	2000	2005	2010
Housing Units Demanded (Based on Employment and Countywide Jobs-per-Housing Ratio)					
CAA 41	54,144	54,358	52,973	54,416	55,622
CAA 44	35,387	37,611	36,949	35,985	36,026
Total	86,532	91,968	89,922	90,401	91,648
Existing/Projected Housing Units					
CAA 41	21,439	21,773	01,903	22,329	22,756
CAA 44	21,814	23,286	24,050	24,235	24,419
Total	43,253	45,059	45,953	46,564	47,175
Housing Demand Not Met within CAA 41 and CAA 44	43,279	46,909	43,969	43,837	44,473
SCTC's Share of Housing within CAA 41 and CAA 44	5.69%	6.90%	7.73%	7.82%	7.88%
SCTC's Share of Unmet Demand	2,462	3,236	3,399	3,428	3,505
Increase in Unmet Demand	2,462	773	163	29	77
Housing Growth Projected		647	444	89	77
Total Potential (Unmet Demand + Projected Growth)	2,462	1,420	607	118	154
Cumulative Potential Demand	2,462	3,883	4,490	4,608	4,762

Source: Orange County Preferred Projections 1992 modified.

ment. Figure 5-23 presents a calculation of the sale prices and rents that would have to be achieved for development to be feasible at various densities and land values. It is assumed that as densities increase, construction costs increase per square foot and unit sizes decrease. Densities range from 30 to 90 units per acre, the latter the highest density that can be achieved with typical wood frame construction over parking. Densities of 90 units per acre require two levels of parking covering the entire site, with four floors of wood frame apartments above. Units average 700 to 800 square feet. Land values range from $25 per square foot ($1.1 million per acre) to $100 per square foot ($4.4 million per acre). At $100 per square foot, land costs would run $50,000 per unit, assuming 90 units per acre.

For condominiums to be feasible, sale prices must be between $150,000 and $350,000. Taking the middle values for each variable, the minimum sale price for a 925-square-foot condominium must be $194,000.

A similar calculation is used to estimate rents. It is assumed that apartments would have a lower level of finish and amenities and thus would be less expensive to build. Using simple capitalization, rents must be between $1,200 and $3,600 per month. It is likely that apartments would be built only if densities of 50 units per acre or greater can be achieved and land can be purchased for about $25.00 to $50.00 per square foot. (These prices and rents exceed typical market prices and rents today and thus might not be achievable in the current market.)

About 40 percent of the households with workers employed at South Coast Town Center thus could likely afford market-rate ownership housing, and about 50 percent could afford market-rate apartments. Assuming a 50/50 mix of apartments and condominiums, about 45 percent of South Coast Town Center's workers could afford to live in the core.

Figure 5-21
Household Size of All Households, by Distance of Residence from South Coast Town Center

	Census Tract 63907	2-Mile Radius*	2–5 Miles	5–10 Miles	Weighted Average
Households with One Person	32%	24%	19%	20%	20%
Households with Two Persons	36%	31%	28%	32%	31%
Households with Three or Four Persons	25%	28%	31%	33%	32%
Households with Five or More Persons	7%	17%	22%	14%	17%

*Includes Tract 63907.

Note: Columns might not add to 100 percent because of rounding.

Source: 1990 Census of Population and Housing.

Estimate of Likely Demand

In estimating the total housing needs of the area's employees, it is useful to look at a regional jobs-per-housing ratio. As mentioned earlier, increasingly many of Orange County's workers live outside the county, so that the county's jobs-per-housing ratio is an understatement of the county's real needs. SCAG estimates that the jobs-per-housing ratio in 1990 was 1.31 and projects that the ratio will decline to 1.22 by 2010.

Using a regional ratio, South Coast Town Center currently generates the need for 22,073 housing units, based on current employment. As employment increases, the housing needs generated by South Coast Town Center will increase, to 29,943 (see Figure 5-24). Given that 22.5 percent of South Coast Town Center's workforce would be suited and eligible to live in the type of housing that could feasibly be built at South Coast Town Center (based on household size and income), South Coast Town Center's fair share should be scaled down by 77.5 percent, to 4,966 housing units.

South Coast Town Center today contains about half the housing units estimated to be needed—2,461 housing units in the area. Presumably this "capture rate" of housing needs reflects residential preferences and the availability of attractive, reasonably priced housing in the area. As noted earlier, South Coast Town Center attracts less than its share of very-high-income households (those with incomes over $150,000 per year).

If one assumes that, in the future South Coast Town Center will continue to provide housing units at the same rate relative to the total amount of housing needs generated by its workers, the potential exists for another 877 housing units between 1990 and 2010, primarily as a result of employment growth. This projection is lower than the 1,257 housing units that the county projects will be added to the housing stock between 1990 and 2010.

If one assumes that South Coast Town Center's appeal as a residential location will improve as workers look for alternatives to longer commutes and enough high-density housing is built to support local services, then the ratio of housing units to the number of eligible households might increase. Figure 5-24 projects housing demand based on an assumption that South Coast Town Center might increase its capture rate to 70 percent by 2010, about 1,000 units more than the county has projected.

Whether this second scenario is likely to occur will depend on whether or not housing policies permit high-density housing to be built at moderate prices, so that the area can be a viable mixed-use residential and commercial district offering a full range of local services and amenities.

The Supply Side: Past Experience and Projected Capacity

Factors Encouraging and Limiting the Development of Housing to Meet Demand

Encouraging Factors

State, regional, and local housing policies. The legislated involvement of state, county, and local authorities to implement housing policy is an important factor encouraging increased housing. In 1980, the state of California amended the Government Code by adding Article 10.6 regarding housing elements. In effect, the state declared that ". . . the availability of housing is of vital statewide importance and the early attainment of decent housing and a suitable living environment for every California family is a priority of the highest order." The state went

▼ ▼

Figure 5-22
Distribution of Estimated Household Income and Affordable Housing for Workers at South Coast Town Center

Number of Workers: 24,486

Household Income	Percent of Total*	Maximum Affordable Rent**	Maximum Affordable House Price***
Less than $12,5000	2.56	$313	$44,400
$12,500–14,999	2.27	$344	$48,800
$15,000–17,499	2.81	$406	$57,700
$17,500–19,999	2.65	$469	$66,500
$20,000–22,499	3.58	$531	$75,400
$22,500–24,999	3.04	$594	$84,300
$25,000–27,499	3.79	$656	$93,200
$27,500–29,999	3.09	$719	$102,000
$30,000–32,499	4.39	$781	$110,900
$32,500–34,999	2.97	$844	$119,800
$35,000–37,499	3.97	$906	$128,700
$37,500–39,999	2.97	$969	$137,500
$40,000–42,499	4.10	$1,031	$146,400
$42,500–44,999	2.92	$1,094	$155,300
$45,000–47,499	3.49	$1,156	$164,100
$47,500–49,999	2.78	$1,219	$173,000
$50,000–54,999	6.44	$1,313	$186,300
$55,000–59,999	5.15	$1,438	$204,100
$60,000–74,999	13.07	$1,688	$239,600
$75,000–99,999	12.19	$2,188	$310,500
$100,000–124,999	5.59	$2,813	$399,300
$125,000–149,999	2.27	$3,438	$488,000
$150,000 or More	3.90	$5,000	$709,800
	100.00		

Median Income: $48,751

*Income distribution based on 1990 Census data for employees in Census Tract 63907.
**Maximum rent assumed to be 30 percent of household income.
***Housing budget for owned housing assumed to be as follows:
Downpayment: 20 percent of purchase price
Mortgage payment: 25 percent of household income
Interest rate: 8 percent per year
Term: 30-year amortization.
Sources: 1990 Census of Population and Housing; authors' estimates.

▲ ▲

Figure 5-23
Housing Prices and Rents at Different Densities and Land Values

Condominium Prices:

	Sale Prices at Assumed Land Value of:		
Density (Units per Acre)	$25 per Square Foot	$50 per Square Foot	$100 per Square Foot
30	$224,324	$267,029	$352,441
50	$168,454	$194,078	$245,325
90	$146,588	$160,824	$189,294

Assumptions	Density (Units per Acre)	Unit Size (Square Feet)	Hard Cost* (Per Square Foot)
Soft Costs: 25% of hard cost	30	1,300	$95
Developer's Profit: 15% of sale price	50	925	$105
	90	750	$120

Apartment Rents:

	Monthly Rent at Assumed Land Value of:		
Density (Units per Acre)	$25 per Square Foot	$50 per Square Foot	$100 per Square Foot
30	$1,986	$2,519	$3,587
50	$1,456	$1,776	$2,417
90	$1,234	$1,412	$1,767

Assumptions	Density (Units per Acre)	Unit Size** (Square Feet)	Hard Cost*** (Per Square Foot)
Soft Costs: 25% of hard cost	30	975	$81
Developer's Profit: 15% of project's value	50	694	$89
Expenses and Vacancy: 40% of potential gross income	90	563	$102
Cap Rate: 9% of net operating income			

*Source: C.C. Mow, president, Century West.
**75 percent of condominium unit size.
***85 percent of condominium unit cost per square foot.

on further to make clear that doing so requires the co-operation of public and private sectors "in an effort to expand housing opportunities and accommodate the housing needs of Californians of all economic levels. . . . " It further emphasized that "local and state governments have a responsibility to use the powers vested in them to facilitate the improvement and development of housing to make adequate provision for the housing needs of all economic segments of the community."

The state became a motivator behind programs designed to encourage housing plans and initiatives in individual communities, and it is a driving force behind much of the city planning that has incorporated housing designed to benefit every economic segment of the population.

In 1982, the state published the California Housing Plan, with its five major themes:
1. Increasing the supply of new houses;
2. Reducing the costs of new houses;
3. Locating housing close to jobs;
4. Preserving existing housing and neighborhoods; and
5. Assisting consumers and special population groups.

In 1990, the state issued the California Statewide Housing Plan Update, with its four goals:

Figure 5-24

Housing Demand Summary for South Coast Town Center

	1990	2000	2010
Estimated and Projected Employment	28,915	32,638	36,530
Regional Jobs-per-Housing Ratio	1.31	1.27	1.22
SCTC's Fair Share of Housing Units	22,073	25,699	29,943
Percentage of One- and Two-Person Households	50.00	50.00	50.00
Percentage of Households Who Could Afford New Housing at SCTC	45.00	45.00	45.00
Eligibility Rate (Combination of These Two Factors)	22.50	22.50	22.50
Number of Eligible Households (SCTC's Fair Share × Eligibility Rate)	4,966	5,782	6,737
Demand, Assuming SCTC Maintains Its Current Capture Rate			
Market Capture: Ratio of Housing Units to Eligible Households	49.55%	49.55%	49.55%
Demand for Housing Units	2,461	2,865	3,338
Existing Housing Units (1990)	2,461		
Unmet Demand	0		
Future Demand from Employment Growth		404	473
Cumulative Demand for Additional Housing Units	0	404	877
Demand, Assuming SCTC Increases Its Current Capture Rate			
Market Capture: Ratio of Housing Units to Eligible Households	55.00%	62.50%	70.00%
Demand for Housing Units	2,731	3,614	4,716
Existing Housing Units (1990)	2,461		
Unmet Demand	270		
Future Demand from Employment Growth		883	1,102
Cumulative Demand for Additional Housing Units	270	1,153	2,255

Sources: Southern California Association of Governments; Orange County Forecast and Analysis Center; authors' estimates.

1. Developing new housing;
2. Preserving existing housing;
3. Reducing the cost of housing; and
4. Improving housing conditions for groups with special needs.

The implementation of state legislation is carried out by regional policy makers—in the case of the selected area, by the Southern California Association of Governments, which is responsible for policies covering the six-county southern California region. SCAG prepared the Regional Housing Needs Assessment (RHNA) to analyze areawide housing needs and conditions, and a fair-share distribution mechanism to assign responsibility for meeting a percentage of the area's low- and moderate-income housing needed in each jurisdiction. SCAG designed the Areawide Housing Opportunity Plan (AHOP) to promote greater freedom of choice in housing. It allows local governments to act in concert to distribute housing funds and promote housing opportunities within a regional/local formula rather than a federal one. "Regional Housing Element" is an advisory document designed to assist individual communities with their problems regarding housing; it focuses on the areas of relationships in housing development, housing needs and production, renovation, affordable housing, discrimination against minorities, and the separation of jobs from housing opportunities.

SCAG's RHNA reveals that a demand for housing exists in all the cities of the region and that housing for greater numbers of lower-income households and higher-density residential development are needed. According to SCAG, approximately 124,000 housing units must be constructed every year throughout the SCAG region just to house the regional population anticipated in 1994.

As part of the implementation plan for the regional housing element, communities are directed to "provide adequate funding for low- and moderate-income housing assistance programs and to provide housing opportunities for lower-income households in all major geographical areas of the region."

For the county, the current housing element focuses primarily on the unincorporated areas under county jurisdiction; it contains an analysis of county housing needs and a comprehensive problem-solving strategy with implementation.

State and county involvement in setting housing goals and objectives as high priorities is a fundamental motivation for individual communities to produce guidelines, goals, and objectives of their own for housing needs. In 1969, local governments first began to include a housing element in their general plans. Today, Costa Mesa and Santa Ana have detailed housing policies incorporated into their general plans that address many of the same policy issues emphasized by the state and county, in turn providing an additional reference point for the development of community-based housing programs.

The city of Costa Mesa has been instrumental in the placement of approximately 2,501 new housing units, 1,763 of which were built since 1987, and the rehabilitation of 268 low- and moderate-income housing units since 1980, using community development block grant funds. Within the study area, The Lakes project rents 20 percent of its units to tenants who earn less than 80 percent of the city's median income. The city of Santa Ana forecasts the completion of 1,236 new housing units (including 808 assisted affordable units) by June 1999, including 511 (451 assisted affordable units) by June 1994. None of the past projects in Santa Ana are part of the study area, however. Further, no affordable housing units inside the study area are currently under construction or about to start, either in Santa Ana or Costa Mesa.

Sectoral diversity and employment growth. The existing strength and forecast growth in the service, retail, and manufacturing sectors support the development of new housing and are key resources for business and industry that could possibly lead to further economic expansion. With the exception of the recession in the early 1990s, the selected area shows employment growing faster than the supply of housing necessary to accommodate the labor pool. A continued housing shortage could drive workers out of the area, resulting either in a decline in the area's economic health or additional negative transportation effects as more workers must commute from outside the area.

Private development of underdeveloped properties. Private development of underdeveloped properties or the conversion of existing older dwelling units and mobile homes is a possibility for future high-density residential growth in the area. Redevelopment is more likely to occur spontaneously when the following factors occur:
1. Developable land is scarce;
2. Developed properties are older and become prime targets for removal;
3. The cost of new development outside the subcenter increases; and
4. Rents, sale prices, and land values increase rapidly.

In anticipation of conversions from single-family to multifamily units and from apartments to condominiums, both Costa Mesa and Santa Ana have adopted land use and zoning strategies that tend to discourage redevelopment except for low- and moderate-income housing. Because such housing requires significant public subsidies, it is limited by budgetary constraints, if not by official policy.

Strategies to discourage redevelopment are motivated by a desire to protect single-family housing in the area and by the slow-growth movement. Costa Mesa enacted policies reserving discretionary right to reject proposals to convert rental apartments into for-sale condominiums in the event of a rental shortage or vacancy rate of 3 percent or lower.

Regulatory incentives. Many traditional incentives are offered to developers to build low- and moderate-income housing (which can translate into high-density residential units). The incentives take several forms:
1. Public redevelopment and assistance;
2. Zoning for planned residential developments or specific developments;
3. Concurrent applications and fast-tracking for zoning approvals, permits, and variances that help to streamline entitlement processing;
4. Density bonuses;
5. Fee reductions and exemptions.

To increase housing in a manner consistent with the goal of preventing the intrusion of multifamily structures into single-family neighborhoods, the city of Santa Ana is developing changes to its single-family standard lot (currently a minimum of 6,000 square feet). The changes allow smaller lots for single-family units, attached single-family houses, and zero-lot-line developments.

The housing element of Santa Ana's 1989 General Plan designates four high-density district centers that allow up to 90 units per acre. One of the designated district centers is located adjacent to the study area in Santa Ana at Hutton Center and MacArthur Place. If the designation is finalized, this district center would provide sufficient density to catalyze residential development in that part of Santa Ana adjacent to the Town Center.

Limiting Factors

Slow growth. The single most obvious obstacle to the development of higher-density housing is the widespread slow-growth attitude that permeates politics. Slow growth is the prevailing sentiment of the region, and new development is likely to meet resistance from both planning agencies and local community groups. An underlying belief exists that more growth leads to traffic, crime, and blight and will make the area more similar to the Los Angeles area. Voters and elected officials do not want more high-density housing and do not actively encourage it, even though policy provisions exist within overall regional plans to incorporate the necessary housing. The city of Costa Mesa hired Opinion Research to survey residents' attitudes as part of its update of the General Plan. Seventy-nine percent of those surveyed thought the city should limit the number of apartments and condominiums, and 69 percent viewed this type of development as a serious issue.

The development community, on the other side, contends that the current political and social environment is poisoned with slow-growth sentiment, matched by misplaced priorities with regard to development and traffic.

Misplaced priorities. The basic conflict among developers, public agencies, and the community in the selected subcenter seems to be an issue of priorities. Priorities, at least in a political context, have shifted within the subcenter from attention to growth, development, and jobs to a preoccupation with controlling and limiting traffic congestion in the area.

Several prominent developers and landowners interviewed for this study expressed concern that the local government and community have placed traffic improvement much higher on the list of priorities than development, growth, and jobs. They claim that the local government's solution to traffic congestion is downzoning, traffic impact fees, and other forms of development exactions. They believe that these misplaced priorities are the effect of regional problems and the impact of Proposition 13, deliberately aimed at reducing development. They predict a loss of jobs as a result of restrictions on development in general—restrictions imposed by tightening regulations—and a scenario for the subcenter that is static without any clear-cut vision for growth. Even if the economy were different, developers could not profitably develop a residential product in the study area because of the current zoning and politics.

Measure M. The shift in emphasis from development and housing to traffic is underscored by the passage of a growth management ordinance, Measure M, in April 1992. The imposition of an additional half-cent sales tax, as dictated by Measure M, goes directly to funding countywide transportation projects, including widening certain streets, improving overall highway conditions, completing longstanding freeway projects, and implementing a rapid-transit system in the near future.

Measure M found favor with the voters because the region is already perceived as unable to handle the amount of traffic that flows into and out of it daily. The underlying sentiment originating from the voters is that new development, including housing (and especially high-density housing), should be discouraged. Measure M includes a provision to assess impact fees on new development to mitigate the effects of new traffic and transportation problems that the development might cause. With the emphasis shifting to traffic and growth management and the concomitant assessment of more fees on development, the incentive to develop is lowered.

The development community and the political leadership in the subcenter are at odds over the priority placed on traffic congestion. The development community maintains that higher-density residential use within a mixed-use development or mixed-use area mitigates traffic congestion and creates a synergy resulting from proximity and layering of use. The development community and the current political leadership not only disagree over what should take priority—new development or traffic problems—but also view the possible solution to traffic problems from opposite positions.

A centerpiece of SCAG's strategies to reduce congestion throughout the metropolitan area is the balance between jobs and housing. SCAG seeks to encourage housing development in and around major employment centers to reduce the distance that workers commute to work.

Cost and availability. Rapid job growth in the South Coast Town Center has combined with limited new housing in the area to increase congestion. The housing that is built tends to be priced above $300,000 because of the high cost of land, lengthy entitlement processes, and limitations on density.

The lack of sufficient housing to satisfy demand closer to South Coast Town Center is affected by a number of other factors as well: demand associated with new immigrants, decreasing household sizes, increasing household formations, the lack of suitable vacant sites, the overall inflation rate, and the cost of labor, land, and materials.

According to the city of Costa Mesa, the cost of single-family houses in the region tripled between April 1970 and April 1979. The rate of increase slowed, but the average price increased by approximately 50 percent from

1979 to 1985. Housing prices increased another 35 percent from 1986 to 1988, with an 8 percent drop reported in 1991 as a result of the recession. In 1986, the median sale price of new houses in Orange County was $171,000; by 1990 it had increased to nearly $250,000. The *Los Angeles Times* reports that the price dropped to $230,000 in 1991. Though the recent recession has contributed to a drop in the price of new houses, a high demand still exists compared to a limited supply of housing in the region.

According to a January 1979 study by *Building Standards* magazine, construction costs in 1979 ranged from $27.60 to $36.40 per square foot for single-family units and from $26.00 to $31.60 per square foot in multifamily units. By 1991, the cost increased from $51.50 to $72.90 per square foot for single-family units and $49.80 to $76.80 per square foot for apartments, representing 45 percent of the total housing cost. According to the city of Costa Mesa, land costs $33,000 to $50,000 per acre for single-family houses and $13,100 to $25,400 per acre for multi-family housing, representing 20 to 30 percent of total housing costs. The city says that, according to a 1991 appraisal, the average value of residential land is $80,000 per single-family unit and $50,000 to $70,000 per multi-family unit.

Heterogeneous land use policies. The region has established a desire to limit the amount of high-density housing that is built close to low-density housing. These objectives correlate higher-density housing directly with higher traffic generation and indirectly with the adverse effects that higher density creates on existing public transportation systems, utility services, schools, and other city services.

The regional emphasis is decidedly in favor of encouraging owner-occupied housing (as opposed to rental units); it is clearly an economic-based measure, as owners are deemed more economically desirable than renters for the region's long-term prosperity. The city of Costa Mesa's 1992 General Plan, for example, cut in half the FAR for commercial development and dwelling units per acre for high-density housing in favor of encouraging lower-density development and consistency with owner-occupied housing.

"Beggar-thy-neighbor" impacts. It is well known that significant impacts to housing in one city result from the enactment of local growth management policies and exclusionary zoning policies in surrounding cities. The aggressive commercial development in the study area in and around South Coast Plaza promoted by the city of Costa Mesa paralleled by restrictions on residential density gave rise to a residential market and demand for higher-density housing in neighboring Santa Ana, where housing development was less restricted. This failure to coordinate growth management policies across jurisdictions continues to limit the development of housing.

Government regulations. State and local government regulations can affect the supply of housing through land use controls, building codes, development and impact fees, project processing fees, onsite and offsite improvements, zoning code requirements, and environmental review. State and county housing policy requires cities to be responsible for reviewing and modifying constraints on housing growth so as not to interfere with the supply, distribution, and cost of housing. The development community contends that the current environment has constrained new medium- and high-density residential development in the study area, citing recent reductions in units per acre and FARs as evidence of these constraints. Before adoption of the new General Plan in Costa Mesa in 1992, an "urban residential" zone of 50 dwelling units per acre existed. It was dropped in the new General Plan, and other land use categories were downzoned as follows:

Density	Dwelling Units per Acre	
	Before 1992	After 1992
High-Density Residential	15–30	12–20
Medium-Density	8–14	8–11

The new ceiling for high-density residential development is too low for residential use to be even remotely competitive with nonresidential uses in the Town Center.

Jurisdictional barriers. Interviews with both Costa Mesa and Santa Ana officials point to clear jurisdictional barriers that impede a comprehensive approach to increasing housing in the study area. The division of power associated with jurisdictional boundaries results in a spirit of territorial protectionism and a general unwillingness to effect development for the common good. Reliance on multiagency entities like SCAG to resolve microregional development issues is not sufficient, because they have limited power to enforce policies for local municipalities.

In addition, Proposition 13 continues to affect each city's financial resources, in turn limiting the ability to implement cohesive development policy within a city, let alone across jurisdictions. Proposition 13 limits property taxes to 1 percent of the real estate sale price and restrains cities from raising taxes without a majority of two-thirds of the voters. The side effects of Proposition 13 include limitations on city-provided services, deteriorating infrastructure, and ever-increasing development exactions. Mello-Roos Special Facilities Districts, redevelopment, and joint powers agreements are among the few approaches available to make up the revenue gap and to ease the burden of development exactions.

The Performance of Various Types of Housing

The housing stock at South Coast Town Center has followed the pattern of the communities of which it is a part. The area contains tracts of single-family housing that were developed in the 1960s and 1970s. The housing there is relatively small and modest compared to the larger, more expensive houses that were built in other parts of the county during the 1980s. More recent development at South Coast Town Center has been almost entirely higher-density, multifamily housing, primarily apartments, with a relatively high level of amenities. Projects currently proposed to be built in the area are entirely multifamily units.

In the assessment of the relative performance of rental and for-sale housing, the authors obtained data from the Orange County Apartment Association, which tracks apartment inventory, rents, and vacancies, and from DataQuick, which tracks inventory, sales, and prices of for-sale housing. They also identified the major apartment complexes in the study area and interviewed the managers or leasing agents to find out about designs, units, rents, tenant profiles, and competitive position of each project.

Vacancies in the South Coast Metropolitan Area and Orange County

Figure 5-25 shows vacancies for the South Coast metropolitan area for the spring quarter in 1992 and 1993. (The metropolitan area includes parts of Santa Ana and Costa Mesa around the Town Center.) Vacancies rose from 1992 to 1993.[2] Figure 5-26 shows how vacancies in Costa Mesa compared to those in other cities in Orange County in 1992. The Costa Mesa area, compared to the surrounding neighborhoods, has one of the lowest vacancy rates.

A comparison of South Coast metropolitan vacancies with surrounding neighborhoods makes it obvious that a strong demand exists for high-density types of housing. A breakdown of unit size and prices helps arrive at a better understanding of the market demand.

Figure 5-27 shows total vacancies by size of unit for the Orange County area. Relatively little difference exists in the vacancy rate based on unit size, although studio apartments have a slightly lower vacancy rate than larger units (4.9 percent for studio apartments versus 5.6 percent for three-bedroom units). Furnished units of all sizes have twice the vacancy of unfurnished units of the same size. And the highest vacancies are found in the oldest apartments. Almost half the apartments (49 percent) are two-bedroom units; 39 percent are one-bedroom units.

Figure 5-25
Costa Mesa Rental Survey (Spring 1992 and Spring 1993)

Year	Percent Vacant	Total Properties Surveyed	Total Units	Total Vacant Units
1992	3.2	142	5,477	393
1993	5.7	183	4,602	262

▲ ▲

Studio apartments and three-bedroom units each account for about 6 percent of Orange County's total stock.

Figure 5-28 breaks down vacancies by price range and age for Orange County. Prices range from $500 to $1,101 per month and up, vacancies from 20 percent to nothing. The study area encompasses many different types of apartment complexes. By breaking the number of units available down to a micro level, it is possible to see the vacancy rates for apartments by size and price range. Surprisingly, vacancy rates tend to be higher for lower-rent apartments. Most of such units, however, are in parts of Orange County outside the study area.

Figure 5-29 shows the total number of units available for the Costa Mesa area.

Apartments in the Study Area

On a micro level, six apartment complexes were surveyed in the immediate study area. The apartments are diverse. Some are quiet, catering to businesspeople who want to live in a parklike setting; others cater to swinging singles and college students. Information on their rental rates and unit sizes is shown in Figure 5-30.

The Lakes apartment complex. Many people consider The Lakes apartment development the swinging singles place in the South Coast metropolitan area. Monthly rents for The Lakes range from $750 to $1,445. Average floor area is 1,053 square feet, with a total of 770 units in the complex. The Lakes has the highest density of all the complexes surveyed. Its amenities range from indoor recreation facilities to private tennis lessons from the on-staff tennis pro. Other amenities include video rentals and dry cleaning. A monthly newsletter and social calendar is published for the residents. Social events planned by the management are available every night. According to the leasing manager, two-bedroom units are the easiest to rent. Rent concessions of $50 to $100 per month off the nominal rent are available.

Versailles. Versailles-On-The-Lake apartments have a different ambience, and apartments are marketed as

Figure 5-26
Apartment Vacancies in Orange County

Zip Code	City	All Units			Over 25 Years			6–25 Years			Fewer than 6 Years		
		Percent Vacant	Total Units	Number Vacant	Percent Vacant	Total Units	Number Vacant	Percent Vacant	Total Units	Number Vacant	Percent Vacant	Total Units	Number Vacant
92801-17	Anaheim	7.1	6,389	454	8.2	2,556	210	6.9	3,087	212	4.3	746	32
92620-21	Brea	5.9	1,022	60	5.8	69	4	6.7	536	36	4.8	417	20
90602-21	Buena Park	8.9	597	53	9.1	372	34	6.5	217	14	62.5	8	5
92629-27	**Costa Mesa**	**3.2**	**3,082**	**98**	**5**	**713**	**36**	**2.7**	**1,523**	**41**	**2.5**	**846**	**21**
90630	Cypress	14.3	35	5	0	10	0	20	26	5	0	0	0
92629	Dana Point	7.5	428	32	0	0	0	2.9	35	1	7.9	393	31
92780	Fountain Valley	7.4	862	64	0	10	0	7.4	851	63	100	1	1
92631-33	Fullerton	5.1	1,235	62	10.5	181	19	4.1	1,022	42	3.2	32	1
92640-44	Garden Grove	5.2	1,302	68	6.5	463	30	4.5	839	38	0	0	0
92645-49	Huntington Beach	4.7	1,792	85	5.9	136	8	4.8	1,574	75	2.4	82	2
92713-20	Irvine	3.3	7,885	259	0	0	0	3.2	7,482	239	5	403	20
90632	La Harba	6.6	670	44	9	178	16	5.7	492	28	0	0	0
92651-6-77	Laguna Beach	6.3	1,797	114	15.4	26	4	6.3	603	38	6.2	1,158	72
92630	Lake Forest	3.0	1,302	39	0	0	0	3.6	886	32	1.7	416	7
90720	Los Alamitos	5.7	53	3	10.3	29	3	0	24	0	0	0	0
92691-92	Mission Viejo	2.0	1,031	21	0	0	0	1.8	502	9	2.3	527	12
92658-63	Newport Beach	4.4	3,117	136	3.1	98	3	4.4	3,019	133	0	0	0
92665-69	Orange	6.7	1,156	78	12	216	26	5.8	868	60	2.8	72	2
92670	Placentia	4.8	900	48	14.3	35	5	5.7	490	28	2.7	375	10
92672	San Clemente	3.8	471	18	5.9	51	3	10.4	48	5	2.7	372	10
92701-12	Santa Ana	7.4	3,695	273	11	543	60	6.9	3,018	209	2.9	136	4
90880	Stanton	9.1	176	16	17.6	17	3	8.2	158	13	0	0	0
92680	Tustin	5.5	2,727	151	2.6	194	5	7.5	1,260	94	4.1	1,283	52
92883	Westminster	6.3	543	34	5.6	250	14	6.8	293	20	0	0	0
92686	Yorba Linda	6.3	16	1	0	0	0	6.3	16	1	0	0	0
	Total	5.2	42,283	2,216	7.9	6,147	483	4.9	28,869	1,436	4.2	7,267	302

Source: Orange County Apartment Association fall rental survey, 1992.

part of a community. Residents are assured of "extremely quiet" residential living 24 hours a day. Built on 18 acres, this community is centered around a 5.5-acre lake. Many of the apartments overlook the lake and offer excellent views. Density is 20 dwelling units per acre. Other amenities that set Versailles apart are a $\frac{4}{5}$-mile jogging path around the complex and corporate suites. All units can be rented fully furnished upon request. Concessions range from a month's free rent to a low security deposit.

Aspen Village/Santa Fe Village. Aspen Village/ Santa Fe Village is among the most luxurious apartment complexes in the study area. Although some students live there, most of the residents are business and professional people who work in South Coast Town Center and surrounding areas. Tenants work for some of the area's best-known corporate names. Rents average $1,125 per month, and the average unit is 1,010 to 1,106 square feet. The complex is built in a parklike setting. While the amenities are not as strong as in other complexes, rents are comparable. The complex sits on the border of the survey area. Concessions range up to $50 to $100 off quoted monthly rent.

South Coast Racket Club. South Cost Racket Club is located on the north side of Sunflower, between Bristol and Main. The complex is across the street from the Performing Arts Center and The Lakes. Monthly rents

Figure 5-27
Vacancies by Size of Unit in Orange County

	All Units			Over 25 Years			6–25 Years			Fewer than 6 Years		
Size of Rental	Percent Vacant	Total Units	Number Vacant	Percent Vacant	Total Units	Number Vacant	Percent Vacant	Total Units	Number Vacant	Percent Vacant	Total Units	Number Vacant
Total Studios	4.9	2,544	121	10.2	401	41	4.2	1,357	57	2.9	788	23
Furnished	10.8	201	22	13.5	155	21	2.2	46	1	0.0	0	0
Unfurnished	4.2	2,343	99	8.1	246	20	4.3	1,311	56	2.9	788	23
Total 1 Bedrooms	5.1	16,536	836	8.3	2,412	200	4.8	11,521	554	3.0	2,605	82
Furnished	11.5	52	6	11.8	51	8	0.0	1	0	0.0	0	0
Unfurnished	5.0	16,486	830	8.2	2,361	194	4.8	11,520	554	3.0	2,605	82
Total 2 Bedrooms	5.4	20,875	1,124	7.1	2,965	210	5.2	14,251	734	4.9	3,859	180
Furnished	12.7	55	7	17.2	29	5	7.7	26	2	0.0	0	0
Unfurnished	5.4	20,820	1,117	7.0	2,936	205	5.1	14,225	732	4.9	3,859	180
Total 3 Bedrooms	5.6	2,330	131	8.8	373	33	4.7	1,730	81	7.5	227	17
Furnished	5.3	19	1	7.7	13	1	0.0	6	0	0.0	0	0
Unfurnished	5.6	2,311	130	8.9	360	32	4.7	1,724	81	7.5	227	17
Total Furnished	11.0	327	36	13.3	248	33	3.8	79	3	0.0	0	0
Total Unfurnished	5.2	41,960	2,176	7.6	5,930	451	4.9	28,780	1,423	4.2	7,277	302
Grand Total	5.2	42,287	2,212	7.9	6,151	484	4.9	28,859	1,428	4.2	7,277	302

Source: Orange County Apartment Association fall rental survey, 1992.

range from $765 to $1,015, with an average of $890—the second lowest in the study area. According to the manager of the complex, two-bedroom units rent the fastest. Concessions range from $25 to $50 off regular monthly rent, with a flexible deposit required. This complex attracts more families. The rooms and amenities range from average to below-average, compared to the other complexes in the study area.

Park Plaza. The Park Plaza apartment complex is one block south of the South Coast Racket Club. Rents for this complex are the lowest of those surveyed, ranging from $749 to $850 per month, with an average of $800. This complex is the least attractive of the six complexes surveyed in the study area, with below-average amenities. While the rents are the lowest of those surveyed, units average only about 1,000 square feet. The complex is outdated and needs work. It is currently being renovated. Management was willing to make a deal to attract tenants during renovation, and units were available for immediate occupancy.

For-Sale Houses

Although the South Coast metropolitan area consists mostly of apartment complexes, scattered for-sale con-dominiums and single-family tract housing can be found in the area. Most of the apartment complexes were built for future sale as condominiums. All units have built-in washer/dryer hookups and other amenities that would be found in for-sale property. The average sale price for a 1,630-square-foot townhouse was $120,523, while the average house sold for $212,167 and was 1,662 square feet. Figure 5-31 shows a breakdown of for-sale housing in the study area, with data on average square footage and age and a distribution of units by bedrooms and bathrooms.

Alternative Strategies for Increasing Housing in and Around South Coast Town Center

The development community has an uphill battle if it is going to reverse current trends that limit housing opportunities in and around South Coast Town Center. It must attempt to raise housing on the list of priorities and to demonstrate that more housing close to the subcenter

Figure 5-28
Vacancies by Price Range

Rent	All Units Percent Vacant	Total Units	Number Vacant	Over 25 Years Percent Vacant	Total Units	Number Vacant	6–25 Years Percent Vacant	Total Units	Number Vacant	Fewer than 6 Years Percent Vacant	Total Units	Number Vacant
$500 or Less	12.8	406	52	12.6	356	45	14.0	50	7	0.0	0	0
Furnished	13.8	167	23	13.3	165	22	50.0	2	1	0.0	0	0
Unfurnished	12.1	239	29	12.0	191	23	12.5	48	6	0.0	0	0
$501–550	9.6	1,002	95	11.0	601	66	6.7	373	25	14.3	28	4
Furnished	0.0	12	0	0.0	0	0	0.0	12	0	0.0	0	0
Unfurnished	9.6	990	95	11.0	601	66	6.9	361	25	14.3	28	4
$551–600	6.9	2,390	165	9.8	682	67	6.5	1,658	92	11.5	52	6
Furnished	13.3	30	4	13.3	30	4	0.0	0	0	0.0	0	0
Unfurnished	6.6	2,360	161	9.7	652	63	6.5	1,658	92	11.5	52	6
$601–650	6.0	4,879	290	6.9	1,447	100	6.7	3,140	179	3.8	292	11
Furnished	0.0	14	0	0.0	1	0	0.0	13	0	0.0	0	0
Unfurnished	6.0	4,865	290	6.9	1,446	100	5.7	3,127	179	3.8	292	11
$651–700	4.5	4,691	214	7.1	722	51	4.9	2,824	137	2.3	1,145	26
Furnished	10.2	59	6	17.2	29	5	3.3	30	1	0.0	0	0
Unfurnished	4.5	4,632	208	6.6	693	46	4.9	2,794	136	2.3	1,145	26
$701–750	5.6	4,179	220	6.8	662	65	4.9	2,893	143	3.8	314	12
Furnished	9.1	11	1	0.0	3	0	12.5	8	1	0.0	0	0
Unfurnished	5.3	4,168	219	6.8	659	65	4.9	2,885	142	3.8	314	12
$751–800	6.4	4,052	261	5.6	683	38	7.7	2,756	212	1.8	613	11
Furnished	0.0	4	0	0.0	3	0	0.0	1	0	0.0	0	0
Unfurnished	6.4	4,048	281	5.6	680	38	7.7	2,755	212	1.8	613	11
$801–850	5.0	3,354	167	8.5	141	12	5.1	2,161	111	4.2	1,052	44
Furnished	14.3	7	1	25.0	4	1	0.0	3	0	0.0	0	0
Unfurnished	5.0	3,347	166	8.0	137	11	5.1	2,158	111	4.2	1,052	44
$851–900	6.0	4,916	247	8.3	60	5	4.9	3,742	182	5.4	1,114	60
Furnished	20	5	1	20.0	5	1	0.0	0	0	0.0	0	0
Unfurnished	6.0	4,911	246	7.3	55	4	4.9	3,742	182	5.4	1,114	60
$901–950	5.4	1,827	99	6.8	264	18	6.0	669	40	4.6	894	41
Furnished	0.0	5	0	0.0	4	0	0.0	1	0	0.0	0	0
Unfurnished	5.4	1,822	99	6.9	260	18	6.0	668	40	4.6	894	41
$951–1,000	5.0	1,587	75	5.8	137	8	4.3	943	41	6.0	487	29
Furnished	0.0	5	0	0.0	1	0	0.0	4	0	0.0	0	0
Unfurnished	5.0	1,582	75	5.9	136	8	4.4	939	41	6.0	487	29
$1,001–1,050	3.4	4,674	158	0.0	6	0	3.2	4,521	146	8.2	147	12
Furnished	0.0	0	0	0.0	0	0	0.0	0	0	0.0	0	0
Unfurnished	3.4	4,674	158	0.0	6	0	3.2	4,521	146	8.2	147	12
$1,051–1,100	4.2	1,089	46	5.0	20	1	7.8	102	8	3.8	967	37
Furnished	0.0	2	0	0.0	1	0	0.0	1	0	0.0	0	0
Unfurnished	4.2	1,087	46	5.3	19	1	7.9	101	8	3.8	967	37
$1,101 and Up	3.7	3,259	120	11.4	70	8	3.4	3,017	103	5.2	172	9
Furnished	0.0	6	0	0.0	2	0	0.0	4	0	0.0	0	0
Unfurnished	3.7	3,253	120	11.8	68	8	3.4	3,013	103	5.2	172	9
Total Furnished	11.0	327	36	13.3	248	33	3.8	79	3	0.0	0	0
Total Unfurnished	5.2	41,960	2,176	7.6	5,903	451	4.9	28,780	1,423	4.2	7,277	302
Grand Total	5.2	42,287	2,212	7.9	6,151	484	4.9	28,859	1,426	4.2	7,277	302

Source: Orange County Apartment Association fall rental survey, 1992.

▼ ▼

Figure 5-29
Average Rental Rates in Costa Mesa

Unit Type	Properties Surveyed	Average Rent
Studio	12	$614
1 BR	23	$664
2 BR	78	$801
3 BR	36	$1,041

Source: Orange County Apartment Association fall rental survey, 1992.

▲ ▲

might help to reduce traffic congestion in the area by reducing commuting to the subcenter. Further, a proactive relationship between the development community and the cities must be achieved to provide viable alternatives for future development consistent with a long-range vision.

Econometric Modeling

To convince the political leadership in Costa Mesa and Santa Ana, solid evidence of the benefits of building housing in and around the subcenter is needed. One approach for producing such evidence is to formulate an econometric model for urban impact analysis.[3] Such a model could be used to analyze different development scenarios for the full range of direct and indirect costs and benefits associated with more housing.

In the near term, the city of Costa Mesa is preparing a specific plan for the study area to readdress its priorities

and growth management. The opportunity exists for the development community, local government, and the local community to jointly assess growth management priorities in terms of not just traffic mitigation, but also increased employment and revenue.

The Sakioka Farms property designated as "Lot 1" and "Lot 2" could serve as a prototype for the introduction of an econometric analysis, because it is a prime area for development and is located within the study area and the proposed specific plan area. George Sakioka believes that an econometric analysis and proactive participation in the specific plan could provide an alternative to nondevelopment because of the restrictive zoning and entitlement process currently in place. The property consists of 40.3 acres zoned for high-density residential development (25 to 35 dwellings per acre) and 33 acres zoned for urban center commercial development (0.50 FAR retail, 0.60 FAR office), respectively.

As a matter of standard planning practice, development of a general and specific plan should take advantage of readily available econometric modeling techniques to clearly assess fiscal and land use impacts.

Private Redevelopment

One possible option proposed by the city of Costa Mesa in its 1992 General Plan is to increase housing in the study area by increasing supply through the private redevelopment of already built-on properties. The lack of available land for new development in the study area and the diminishing benefits of building farther and farther away from the subcenter inevitably lead to redevelopment. It is not unusual, given that past redevelopment has involved replacement of older single-family

▼ ▼

Figure 5-30
Rents and Sizes of Apartments in the Study Area

Apartments	Rents			Floor Area (Square Feet)			Total Units
	Low	High	Average	Low	High	Average	
The Lakes	$750	$1,445	$1,098	700	1,406	1,053	770
South Coast Racket Club	$765	$1,015	$890	700	975	838	256
Versailles	$770	$1,295	$1,033	720	1,300	1,010	364
Aspen Village	$965	$1,280	$1,123	1,012	1,200	1,106	200
Santa Fe Village	$850	$1,400	$1,125	720	1,300	1,010	142
Park Plaza	$749	$850	$800	980	1,020	1,000	249

Source: Personal interviews.

▲ ▲

Figure 5-31
For-Sale Housing in the Study Area

	Condominium/Townhouse			Single-Family House		
	Total	High	Low	Total	High	Low
Properties	2,615			6,672		
Average Sale Price	$120,523	$200,000	$9,000	$212,167	$355,000	$5,500
Number of Sales Last Year	66			233		
Number of Sales in Last 6 Months	42			152		
Owner-Occupied	51%			83%		
Absent Owner	49%			17%		
Average Square Footage	1,063			1,662		
Average Number of Bedrooms	2			3		
Average Number of Bathrooms	2			2		
Average Age	13	27	4	27	88	3
1 BR	625			101		
2 BR	1,264			360		
3 BR	693			3,172		
4 BR	13			2,455		
5 BR	402			0		
1 BA	721			308		
2 BA	1,830			5,561		
3 BA	44			771		
4 BA	0			5		

Source: DataQuick.

units with multifamily development. Recent building applications have proposed demolition of large and functionally obsolete developments to allow for new construction.

Costa Mesa's General Plan suggests that the public sector needs to be more proactive in providing incentives or assistance that will promote redevelopment by the private sector and meet the balance between jobs and housing required. Costa Mesa currently provides incentives project by project, including:

▼ Modified land use regulations: increased density, lot coverage, and height restrictions, or relaxed parking standards;
▼ Redesignation to more inclusive zones; and
▼ Lot combinations.

In addition, amendments to the General Plan, zoning policies, specific plans, and development standards are envisioned as viable mechanisms to facilitate private redevelopment.

Mixed Use

Possibly the most lucrative and accepted solution to the problem of new high-density housing in the study area is mixed-use development. Such development offers diverse solutions for increased urban problems. Direct benefits include reduced vehicle trips and emissions, reduced use of infrastructure, and access to adjacent compatible uses; indirect benefits include less stress resulting from traffic and more productive time for leisure or work.

Existing planned development ordinances provide for the inclusion of complementary uses. Planned Development Residential (PDR) zones allow inclusion of commercial activities as complementary uses, PDC (commercial) zones allow residential and industrial uses, and PDI (industrial) zones permit both commercial and residential uses if they are compatible with other uses allowed. Commercial uses that have been permitted in PDI zones have generally been justified on the basis that they serve the industries in the area and their employees.

The Lakes is an example of a mixed-use development. Adjacent to the South Coast Town Center, The Lakes combines 770 dwelling units, two hotels, and a 22,000-square-foot retail/commercial center, as well as a large, common open area. This combination of residential, commercial, and retail space has been shown to work as an integrated development.

Mixed-use development tends to be more complex than single-use development, especially when the uses are integrated into a single structure. Properly executed, the mixture of uses can add to the profitability of individual uses. Retail development in Houston's Galleria, for example, is estimated to have sales approximately 10 to 15 percent higher than other similar single-use shopping malls because of the hotel and office uses that are part of the complex. But if it is going to work, the cities must actively encourage mixed-use development. Mixed-use projects cannot be allowed to become targets for exactions and excessive impact fees, or developers will continue to build simpler, single-use projects.

Joint Powers–Growth Management Authority

The creation of a joint powers–growth management authority that incorporates both Costa Mesa's and Santa Ana's goals for development for the study area is a potential solution to increasing the amount of housing near the subcenter. In accord with state law (Government Code Section 6502), Costa Mesa and Santa Ana by mutual agreement can jointly exercise any power common to them. Such a joint powers–growth management authority would enable the cities to jointly use resources and generate revenue to promote development while working toward the mutual goals of reducing traffic congestion and solving other joint problems associated with South Coast Town Center.

Joint powers are broad powers, without the legislative controls commonly found in public redevelopment. Joint powers statutes provide opportunities to effect and fund growth, especially in the aftermath of Assembly Bill 1290, which limits public redevelopment powers to generating retail sales taxes to supplement the general fund. Before Assembly Bill 1290, municipalities fought hard to attract retail activity, because sales taxes represented one of the few sources of revenue to augment a city's general fund. A joint powers authority would include the participation of the private sector and could be instru-

mental in promoting public/private partnerships to develop housing in the area.

Although state and county housing policy requires cities to increase housing and SCAG is helpful in implementing and assisting housing proponents in the six-county region, no substitute exists for local bipartisan responsibility for housing development.

General Conclusions

Conclusions are summarized in the following 12 main points:

1. A significant amount of housing exists adjacent to South Coast Plaza in the form of large apartment complexes. Notwithstanding the presence of this housing, the area is very job rich, because nearly 12 jobs exist for each housing unit in the area. Over a larger area, one that extends about three miles north and south of the site, three jobs are available for each housing unit, roughly twice the average for the county as a whole.

2. No real attempt has been made to integrate housing and commercial areas or to create a sense of neighborhood that encompasses both. The housing projects are segregated and self-contained, with internal amenities and a high level of security. South Coast Plaza suffers from a superblock syndrome. Blocks are very large and generally have a single land use; the massive South Coast Plaza, for example, provides regional retail space, while adjacent blocks contain office towers and freestanding hotels. The Nagouchi garden, surrounded on two sides by office towers and two sides by a parking garage, is a contemplative space completely isolated from the surrounding environment. The Performing Arts Center is the only building that begins to create a public, urban character.

3. The condominium market is very weak, so that units built as condominiums are being rented as apartments. Market rents, however, do not justify the high cost and land values of building apartments at this time. Until market conditions improve, little or no additional housing will be built in the area. It is difficult for residential land uses to compete with high land values generated by commercial development.

4. The market for high-density residential development is for the most part limited to small households with moderate to moderately high incomes because of the small units and relatively high production costs. A primary motivation for living in the area is to be close to work.

5. Based on the county's projections of employment growth, a demand for 900 additional housing units will exist in the area if the area maintains its current market share. If the share is increased, the demand for additional housing might increase to about 2,200 units, which would provide about 16 percent of the housing need generated by the area's employment. To achieve that scale of development, densities will need to be increased from those currently permitted by zoning.

6. The county's projection that employment in the area will continue to grow despite policies that limit or discourage housing could be overly optimistic. Without housing to meet the needs of workers, it is not at all clear that the county can continue to add jobs at the rate it projects. Local governments often encourage job-generating land uses, because these uses also generate sales and property taxes. Housing, on the other hand, tends to generate demand for public services and, in most cases, is a fiscal drain. Without housing, however, the coveted land uses might not appear.

7. The limiting factor on the development of additional housing will not be market demand, but entitlement constraints and mitigation measures required by the local jurisdictions that will both reduce the potential supply of housing and increase production costs. To overcome it, developers will have to build a consensus for the notion that increasing housing options near employment centers is a viable technique to mitigate traffic impacts.

8. Serious traffic problems afflict the area, and freeways and arterials are highly congested. Developers need to be proactive in developing solutions to these problems, which affect everyone. The ability of local governments to actively address problems is limited by constraints on funding and their inability to raise revenues through tax increases.

9. Jurisdictional boundaries and competing interests of the affected cities complicate the planning process. A joint powers authority offers an interesting potential for addressing problems jointly and providing financing mechanisms. Regional government (in the form of SCAG) is generally ineffective in imposing regional guidelines and directives on unwilling local governments.

10. True mixed-use projects offer an opportunity for innovative design and a rationale for increasing density based on trip generation. If additional density can be obtained through mixed-use development, land values could be enhanced.

11. Significant housing will require a coherent strategy to create viable residential neighborhoods or districts, which include local-serving retail goods and services, as well as amenities like public open space and recreational facilities.

12. As a matter of urban design, compelling reasons exist for housing in suburban centers. The inclusion of significant amounts of housing will help to keep suburban centers vital 50 years from today and avoid their becoming the sort of office (and hotel) ghettos that plague central cities throughout the country.

How much can the case of South Coast Town Center be generalized to other suburban subcenters? The location and prominence of the subcenter give it somewhat special advantages for attracting high-density housing compared to other suburban modes. The fact that more housing has not been built—and that what has been built is very low density, compared to the 80 to 100 units per acre that one would expect to find—is the result of a political environment in which housing is given a low priority.

South Coast Town Center's political environment is unfortunately its most generalizable feature, at least for southern California. The cities in which demand exists for high-density housing in and around suburban subcenters are the ones most likely to have vocal opposition from neighborhood groups. To the extent that these concerns can be successfully mediated, high-density housing has a future in southern California suburban nodes. Without such agreement, however, the currently allowable housing densities are so low that landowners would be foolish not to wait for commercial or office uses, even in the face of a very depressed market that begs for conversion of land zoned for office uses to residential uses.

References

City of Santa Ana General Plan, Housing Element, revised March 15, 1993.
City of Santa Ana General Plan, Growth Management Element.
City of Santa Ana Comprehensive Housing Affordability Strategy, January 7, 1992.
City of Santa Ana General Plan, 1982.
City of Costa Mesa General Plan, March 1992.
DataQuick.
South Coast Metro Alliance.

Interviews

Linda Hale, senior planner, Santa Ana Planning and Building Agency. Interviewed on September 24, 1993.

Mike Kerr, owner, Westport Company. Interviewed on October 14, 1993.

Colm Macken, vice president of development, Transpacific Development. Interviewed on October 14, 1993.

C.C. Mow, president, Century West Development. Interviewed on December 15, 1993.

Michael Robinson, principal planner, Costa Mesa Planning Department. Interviewed on September 10, 1993.

Malcolm Ross, director of public relations, Segerstrom Development.

George Sakioka, Sakioka Development. Interviewed on October 1, 1993.

Notes

1. The term "Town Center" describes the commercial and retail district concentrated in and around South Coast Plaza. "Town Center" also more narrowly identifies the office area adjacent to South Coast Plaza.

2. The sample differs for the two years. The number of properties surveyed increased from 142 in 1992 to 183 in 1993, while the number of units decreased from 5,477 in 1992 to 4,602 in 1993.

3. The southern California planning model developed by USC's School of Urban and Regional Planning is an example of a family of econometric models that facilitate economic impact analysis of urban development.

Chapter 6

▲ ▲ ▲ ▲ ▲ ▲ ▲ ▲ ▲

Conclusion

The four suburban employment centers examined in this study indicate that demand for additional housing—especially higher-density products—does exist. The case studies further indicate that local land use policies have influenced significantly the nature and quantity of residential units built. And local policies are continuing to affect the supply of housing in each case studied.

Walnut Creek is at one end of the spectrum: over 20 years of local development controls have worked effectively to curtail housing development, especially of affordable and higher-density units. Even today, little land is zoned for higher-density housing. In large part because these past policies restricted housing, the development economics of the present—particularly high land prices—work against the construction of housing.

Southfield falls at the other end of the spectrum: local land use controls in place for three decades have encouraged the development of thousands of multifamily units near this major employment center. Housing production in the Dallas Galleria area has also benefited from permissive development controls—or, perhaps more accurately, from the lack of restrictive controls. While South Coast Town Center boasts a relatively high housing-to-jobs ratio compared with the rest of Orange County, evidence suggests that the production of new housing will be limited by constraints on entitlements.

All of the suburban employment centers studied have shown little success in integrating housing with other land uses, such as retail and office centers. Unlike in traditional center cities, housing in these centers tends to have been built in isolated clusters not easily accessible to public transit or pedestrians. The case studies further suggest that these suburban centers are not being permitted to evolve naturally or in such a way that might eventually allow them to function like the central cities they surround.

The information gleaned from this limited research supports the contention that housing development near most job-rich suburban employment centers is, and will likely continue to be, constrained by local policies as well as by the economics of land development. The results will include longer commutes, increased shortages of affordable housing, and potential shortages of workers—especially those who receive lower wages. To maintain the long-term economic health of suburban employment centers, this research suggests that local agencies should reevaluate their housing policies with the objective of increasing the production of units that a full range of household incomes can afford.